The Plays
of
Menander

THE PLAYS

OF

MENANDER

Edited and Translated by

Lionel Casson

New York: New York University Press

1971

882

To Bluma Trell

Foreword

Menander was one of the greatest names, if not the greatest, in ancient comedy, the Molière of the Greeks and Romans. He was lauded to the skies by their most eminent critics, his plays were staged wherever Greek was spoken for well-nigh four centuries, he was quoted as frequently as we quote Shakespeare. Yet, when the ancient world died, this literary giant died with it—or so it seemed. Not a manuscript of his works, not a manuscript with even one of his plays, turned up in any of the monastery libraries. We knew from descriptions and imitations what kind of plays he composed, we knew that they had fathered a long line of descendants, from the works of Rome's Plautus and Terence through Molière and English Restoration Comedy to some of today's soap opera, but of his actual writings we had no more than pathetic bits and pieces: a few speeches cited by critics or grammarians in one context or another and a random collection of quotable utterances culled from various plays. This was all we knew of Menander —until the year 1905.

In certain parts of Egypt there is almost no rainfall, and the sands there are perennially dry. Documents and papers discarded thousands of years ago can lie under this protective mantle and emerge as intact as the day they were written. Archaeologists have dug up vast numbers of them, ranging from scribblings on torn pieces of scrap to pages from de luxe manuscripts. In 1905 came electrifying news: excavators working on the site of an ancient village in the Fayum had turned up the tattered remnants of a copy of Menander that dated to the fourth or fifth century A.D. It contained but one half of one play, *The Arbitration,* and about one third of two others, *The Woman of Samos* and *She Who Was Shorn,* but to a world that had long ago given up hope of ever reading anything from the hand of the master, this was manna from heaven. Then, some fifty years later lightning struck again in the same spot: a second manuscript was uncovered, this one containing an entire play, *The Grouch.* It had been written toward the end of the third or beginning of the fourth century A.D. Clandestine diggers and not excavators had unearthed it, and in the course of time it was sold through dealers to a Swiss bibliophile. In 1959 the text was published. Even as the volume appeared, a rumor was afloat that the manuscript included still other plays. This turned out to be true, and the remaining pages were published in 1969. They give us a nearly complete version of *The Woman of Samos* and about half of a piece hitherto all but unknown, *The Shield.*

In 1960 I included in my *Masters of Ancient Comedy* all that we then had by Menander. Since that time, the text of *The Grouch* has received much study and has been vastly improved, and our knowledge of Menander's idiom has been deepened. For this edition I have completely revised the translation of *The Grouch,* considerably revised that of *The Woman of Samos* as well as adding the newly discovered portions, and have made a number of changes in *The Arbitration* and *She Who Was Shorn.* The present volume contains, in effect, one complete play *(The Grouch);* one nearly complete *(The Woman of Samos);* two of which we have approximately half of the original *(The Arbitration, The Shield);* and one of which we have about one-third *(She Who Was Shorn).* Considerable portions of other plays (e.g., *The Sicyonian, The Woman Hater*) have been preserved in various battered manuscripts, but none offer enough consecutive complete lines to justify translation.

In these versions I have adhered to the principle I have used all along in translating Greek and Roman comedies, that is, to make these ancient plays sound as much like contemporary comedy as possible and still remain a translator and not an adapter. That meant not only turning them from verse into prose, but a prose that reflects the vocabulary of current, everyday speech. Every line I translated I subjected to a simple test: I read it aloud and asked myself whether it sounded the way a person would express himself in the given situation today. Frequently the original lent itself to translation that satisfied this requirement and that was at the same time a close one; more often, close translation was impossible and I gave the general sense of a passage with no attempt to reproduce the meaning of the individual words; at times I frankly paraphrased. All references that would make sense only to ancient audiences or modern scholars I replaced with some sort of contemporary equivalent. For the ubiquitous oaths and exclamations that invoke the names of Greek deities I substituted modern expressions; I converted talents and drachmas into dollars (allowing for current inflation has made my figures considerably higher than the usual equations); I doctored the jokes where necessary to make them intelligible to today's audiences. Moreover, in line with my aim to make living theater of these plays, I added full stage directions, just as a contemporary playwright would.

My wife, as always, undertook the arduous job of preparing the manuscript for the printer. She ungrudgingly and tirelessly typed and re-typed page after page; I would never have gotten this book to press without her skilled help. My colleague and dear friend, Bluma Trell, unravelled many a crucial point for me as I was preparing the translation, then read the manuscript and saved me from many a blunder. To her this book is affectionately dedicated.

Contents

Introduction

The Origin of Comedy

One morning in March or April of 534 B.C., at the Greater Dionysia, Athens' major festival in honor of the wine god Dionysus, a man named Thespis led a troupe into a primitive theater and the western world's first formal dramatic performance began.

What Thespis presented on that memorable day was an embryonic form of tragedy. Comedy, however, was not far behind; it made its debut at the festival no more than half a century later, in 486 B.C. And in 442 B.C. it became the feature attraction at the Lenaea, Athens' second most important festival for Dionysus.

Both tragedy and comedy came into being as elements in religious ceremony. What is more, during the whole of their creative period, they were never transformed into commercial theater; born out of worship, they continued to be performed under the aegis of the state as part of the offerings on sacred occasions.

The offerings, as it happened, took the form of a competition. The Greeks liked to hold contests during their festivals, to dedicate to their gods, as it were, the superlative human achievement of a championship performance. The athletic games in honor of Zeus that highlighted his great festival at Olympia come immediately to mind. Athenian drama is another example. All the Greek plays that have survived, from Aeschylus' earliest to Menander's latest, were composed to compete for a prize. The state selected the writers of tragedy and comedy who were to take part, arranged for payment of all their expenses, and set up a panel of judges to choose the winner in each category. In each of the two annual festivals just mentioned, the Greater Dionysia, which was held in March or April, and the Lenaea, which was held in January or February, three tragic playwrights as a rule and five comic (during certain periods only three) entered the lists. A small group of citizens, annually chosen anew, served as the board of judges. *The Grouch* concludes with a plea that "The noble goddess of victory be on our side forever"; this is simply Menander's way of putting in his claim for the prize in comedy at the festival involved. The writers, eager to compete as often as possible, composed fresh works for every festival—which helps to explain why, for example, Sophocles and Euripides and Menander and others turned out over one hundred plays. During their lifetimes, when plenty of creative talent to produce new works was available, a play was rarely, if ever, performed more than once at Athens. The repeat performances took place elsewhere, put on by road companies who went on tour all over the Greek world.

Old Comedy

The type of comedy that flourished in Athens down to the end of the fifth century B.C., usually called Old Comedy, was, by and large, topical satire. We know it almost wholly through the eleven preserved pieces by its most famous practitioner, Aristophanes; he had noted rivals, who often took the prize away from him, but their works for some reason failed to survive. Aristophanes' uproariously funny plays are all variations on a deeply serious theme: the health and future of Athens as a state. The subjects he treats were the burning topics of his day: the bitter war between Athens and Sparta that had broken out in 431 B.C., when he was a young man, and went on during most of his lifetime; the effect on politics of corruption in the law courts; the effect on morals of the new tradition-shattering philosophical and educational ideas that were being expressed; the quality of Athens' avant-garde literature. He deals with such matters in a fearless freewheeling fashion, generally devising a wildly fantastic plot as framework and filling it with mad farce, bawdy skits, wisecracks, and vitriolic personal attacks on public figures. His plays are more musical comedy than legitimate comedy. A featured role is given to a chorus that sang and danced, many of the lines assigned to the actors were sung, and the whole script is written in verse of great variety and high quality.

There are indications that Aristophanes' topical farce was not the only comic fare of the time. It seems almost certain that a number of contemporary writers went in for the comedy of character, for humorous delineations of drunkards, misers, and the like. Unfortunately only meager fragments of such works have come down to us.

The End of Old Comedy

In 404 B.C., after twenty-seven years of fighting, the war between Athens and Sparta finally ended in complete victory for Sparta. Athens' empire had vanished, her armed forces had been destroyed, her treasury was empty.

Aristophanes' last two preserved plays, presented about 392 and 388 B.C., show the results of the war. People were in no mood to listen to the merciless criticism that had been the very soul of his greatest plays; in their unhappy circumstances, Athenians wanted to be amused, not lectured. Bowing to the public taste, the playwright turned to the type of comedy mentioned above that some of his rivals had specialized in. He began to poke fun at men's ways in general and not at their behaviour as citizens in a given situation at a given time. Gone were the music and lyrical verse; he wrote in more or less everyday language. As Browning put it in his "Aristophanes' Apology":

Aristophanes
Surmounts his rivals now as heretofore,
Though stinted to mere sober prosy verse—
"Manners and Men," so squeamish gets the world!
No more "Step forward, strip for anapaests!"
No calling naughty people by their names.

Greek New Comedy

Although Athens soon revived politically and economically,
the circumstances that had nourished Old Comedy never returned. From the beginning of the fourth century B.C. on, people became increasingly interested in their lives as individuals
rather than as members of a body politic. Then, in 338 B.C.,
Athens fell under the domination of the kings of Macedon,
and freedom of speech became overnight a thing of the past.
The Athenians and their neighbors, the Greeks of the other
city-states, were no longer the masters of their own fate,
as they had been to a great extent in the fifth century B.C.
What happened to them depended on the ambitions and whims
of a few kings; life was dictated from above and was terribly unsure. When people went to the theater they wanted
to escape from their daily existence. The writers of comedy
responded by going even further along the path Aristophanes
had followed in his last plays, and by the end of the fourth
century B.C. they had created a new type of comedy, Greek
New Comedy. Its purpose was entertainment; its subject was
people; its chief source of humor, gentle mockery of the manners of men. It was still written in verse, but a verse only
slightly elevated above the rhythms of everyday speech. It
swiftly became enormously popular and eclipsed tragedy;
all the available creative effort was now poured into the sock
and no longer the buskin. As far as the history of literature
is concerned, the new form is a greater achievement than Old
Comedy: Old Comedy had come to an end even before the
death of Aristophanes; New Comedy is still very much alive.

Old Comedy was remarkable for the variety and ingenuity
of its comic ideas. New Comedy was remarkable for its same-
ness. Euripides became the darling of the practitioners of the
new form: he had written many a play that was more romantic
melodrama than tragedy, and they drew from these much
inspiration for their plots. Their favorite formula has re-
mained a favorite with writers and audiences ever since: a boy
and a girl in love who are kept apart by some obstacle, even-
tually surmount or remove it and, as the curtain comes down,

are happily united. The world these playwrights chose to portray is small: it is almost exclusively that of Athenian upper middle class households. The *dramatis personae* are equally limited: the fathers of the households, fine and generous, or cantankerous and miserly, or decent but not very bright; their valets, quick-witted and ingenious, or slow and stupid, or sour and aggressive; the sons of the household, who, with no living to earn, have ample time to philander; self-important army men; self-important cooks; courtesans; hangers-on; pimps. Whatever restrictions this narrow range of characters and plots may have imposed, the playwrights of New Comedy were somehow able to pluck chords that met a universal response. Their love-harassed youths, irate fathers, quick-witted servants, and the rest of their casts have triumphantly survived nearly two and a half millennia and still walk the boards of our theaters and move across our movie and television screens.

Menander (ca. 342-291 B.C.)

Menander presented his first play in 321 B.C., and *The Grouch* came very soon after, in 316, winning first prize at the Lenaea. We can only approximate the dates of the other preserved plays: *The Woman of Samos* has some of the marks of early work, while *She Who Was Shorn* and, in particular, *The Arbitration,* seem to be from his mature period.

Menander by no means dominated the field of New Comedy during his lifetime. There were at least two other acknowledged masters, Diphilus and Philemon. As a matter of fact, both were far more successful practicing playwrights than he. They produced, we gather, a more boisterous type of comedy, and this apparently had greater popular appeal. Of the one hundred or so plays that Menander wrote, only eight gained the prize. However, after his death, he swiftly became the favorite of the critics, and his reputation skyrocketed. One critic after another sang his praises. "O Menander! O life! Which of you has copied the other?" rhapsodized Aristophanes of Byzantium, one of the most learned literary pundits of the ancient world. "So long as there are lying slaves, hard-hearted fathers, wicked pimps, and seductive courtesans in the world, Menander will never die!" gushed Ovid, Rome's noted love poet. "In my opinion, a careful reading of Menander by itself suffices to illustrate all my teachings," asserted Quintilian, Rome's perceptive critic and authority on education, "so well has he held up the mirror to every phase of life, so appropriately does he render all incidents and characters and emotions." And Plutarch on the subject of Menander is practically an exercise in adulation: "Menander's charms have made him superlatively satisfying. Of all the great works that Greek has produced, his poetry is the most universally offered in our theatres. . . . He reveals what true skill in language is, entering upon all subjects with a persuasiveness that cannot be resisted and controlling every sound and thought in the repertoire of the Greek tongue. For what worthwhile reason does an educated man go into a theatre except to see Menander?"

Until very recently we had to take the ancient critics at their word. But, thanks to the spectacular discoveries that have been made since 1905 (see Foreword), we now have enough of his writings at our disposal to savor his quality, if not to appreciate his full flavor. We can now at least attempt an answer to a question that has long been troubling: how could Menander have achieved such a towering reputation when his plots and characters were so limited? More particularly, how could ancient critics have singled out trueness to life as his forte when his stock in trade was basically the same romantic stuff that made up so much of Greek New Comedy? It is a pity that, of the two fully preserved plays, one turns out to be a sample of his earliest work; *The Grouch*, with its meager plot and mealy-mouthed morality, is pretty poor. But what of the others? Are they the plays Quintilian and Plutarch had in mind? Each reader will have to judge for himself.

The Heritage of Menander

The Roman writers of comedy, Plautus and Terence, used the plays of Greek New Comedy as the basis for their works. They borrowed the general plots, the cast of characters, and,

in Terence's case, the tone as well. At least four of the preserved plays of Plautus are based on Menander (*The Pot of
Gold, The Twin Bacchises, The Casket, Stichus*), and four
of Terence's (*The Woman of Andros, The Self-Tormentor,
The Eunuch, The Brothers*). These Roman adaptations, in
turn, served as direct source for much of European comedy.
Thus Menander supplied, as it were, the original capital for
the development of the comedy of manners in the West.

Bibliographical Note

I have used the following texts as the basis of my
translations:

> *The Grouch:* E. Handley, *The Dyskolos of Menander.*
> (London, 1965). In a few minor instances I have de-
> parted from Handley's text.

> *The Woman of Samos* and *The Shield:* C. Austin, *Men-
> andri Aspis et Samia. I, Textus; II, Subsidia Interpre-
> tationis.* (Berlin, 1969-1970).

> *The Arbitration* and *She Who Was Shorn:* A. Koerte,
> *Menandri quae supersunt.* 3rd edition. (Leipzig, 1957).

For those interested in further study of Greek New Comedy, the following books will be helpful.

The theater building and play production:

> A. Pickard-Cambridge, *The Theatre of Dionysus in
> Athens.* (Oxford, 1946).

> ———, *The Dramatic Festivals at Athens.* 2nd edition.
> (Oxford, 1968).

> M. Bieber, *The History of the Greek and Roman Theatre.*
> 2nd edition (Princeton, 1961).

> T. Webster, *Greek Theatre Production.* (London, 1956).

> ———, *Monuments Illustrating Old and Middle Comedy.*
> Bulletin of the Institute of Classical Studies, London
> University. Supplement 9 (London, 1960).

————, *Monuments Illustrating New Comedy*. Bulletin of the Institute of Classical Studies, London University. Supplement 24. 2nd edition (London, 1969).

Menander and Greek New Comedy:

P. Legrand, *Daos*. translated by J. Loeb (London, 1917).

T. Webster, *Studies in Menander*. 2nd edition (Manchester, 1960).

————, *Studies in Later Greek Comedy*. (Manchester, 1953).

Roman Adaptations:

G. Duckworth, *The Nature of Roman Comedy*. (Princeton, 1952).

W. Beare, *The Roman Stage*. 3rd edition (New York, 1965).

The Plays
of
Menander

The Grouch

DRAMATIS PERSONAE

CHAEREAS, a young man who makes his way by sponging on his rich friend Sostratus

SOSTRATUS, a wealthy, young Athenian man about town, in love with Cnemon's daughter

PYRRHIAS, servant (slave) of Sostratus

CNEMON, the grouch, a sour-tempered old farmer, father of the girl Sostratus loves

CNEMON'S DAUGHTER

DAVUS, servant (slave) of Gorgias

GORGIAS, a self-reliant, young Athenian farmer, stepson of Cnemon and half-brother of the girl Sostratus loves

SICON, a cook

GETA, Sostratus' father's valet (slave) whose services Sostratus enlists in his own behalf

SIMIKE, an elderly female servant of Cnemon's, his daughter's old nurse

CALLIPPIDES, father of Sostratus

[MYRRHINA, Cnemon's wife, mother of Gorgias by a former marriage]

SCENE

The scene is laid in Phyle, a country district outside Athens. In the center is the entrance to a grotto sacred to the god Pan and his nymphs. On either side are houses, stage right

that of Cnemon, stage left that of Gorgias. The exit on stage
left leads to Athens, that on stage right to the open country
where Cnemon and Gorgias have their fields.

PROLOGUE

*(Out of a doorway made up to look like the entrance to a
cave comes the god Pan. He is the mischievous fellow, goat
from the waist down and man from the waist up except for
goat's ears and horns, whose divine powers include, among
others, that of inspiring lovers. The locale is a more or less
unfrequented spot in Phyle, a country district about thirteen
miles north of Athens, where a well-known sanctuary sacred
to Pan was located.)*

PAN   *(to the audience)*   I want you to imagine that this
     (with a sweeping gesture) is Phyle, near Athens, and that
     this cave I've just come out of is a famous sanctuary of
     the nymphs which belongs to the farmers of Phyle who
     manage to coax crops out of the stones around here. Now,
     the property on my right here belongs to Cnemon. He's
     a man whose one aim is to be anti-men. He's mean to
     everybody, dislikes being with people—being with people
     did I say? He's lived a good many years by now and so far
     he hasn't willingly exchanged a word with anyone in his
     life. The only conversations he ever starts are when he goes
     past my door—and that's only because I'm a neighbor and
     he can't avoid it. I'm convinced he regrets it the next minute.
        Surprisingly enough, considering the sort he is, he took
     a wife. He married a widow right after she had lost her first
     husband and had been left with a son who was still just
     a child at the time. Cnemon led a miserable life with her,
     quarreling with her not only all day but most of the night
     too. They had a daughter. That made things even worse.
     *(Pauses and shakes his head sorrowfully over the fate of a
     child born into such a household.)*
        When the situaiton got as bad as it possibly could and
     her life was nothing but bitterness and hardship, his wife
     left him and went to live with the son she had had by her

first husband. He's owner of a little plot here in the neighborhood, and he barely manages to squeeze enough from it to feed himself, his mother, and a single faithful old servant who once belonged to his father. He's a young man by now, and wise beyond his years; the school of hard knocks is accelerating his education. The old man lives alone with his daughter and an old hag of a servant and spends his days hauling wood, digging, slaving—and hating everyone in turn, beginning with his wife and neighbors here and going right on through to the outskirts of Athens. The girl has gotten this much benefit from the way she's been brought up: she simply doesn't know what it is to do wrong. And she's respected and worshiped me and my nymphs to the point where she's inclined us to make her our special charge. (*Leaning forward and speaking confidentially*) Now, a young fellow whose father owns farmland around here worth a fortune, and who lives in style in the city, went out hunting with his servant and happened to come to this place. And I've made him fall madly in love with the girl. (*Straightens up and pauses for a moment to let what he has just said sink in.*)

Those are the salient points. The details you'll see if you care to stay—and please care! (*Looking off toward the wings, stage left*) Well, I think I see our young lover and somebody with him coming this way. They're talking about how he fell in love.

ACT I

(*Sostratus and Chaereas enter, stage left. Sostratus is a fine-looking young man dressed in an elaborate hunting costume that obviously cost a good deal of money. He has an open, candid countenance, the sort that inspires immediate confidence, and an eager and enthusiastic temperament that is particularly appealing. It is clear from his manner at the moment that something significant has happened to him to which he has reacted strongly, as one of his nature would. His companion is totally different. He is also young but there is nothing open in his nature. He is, as a matter of fact, a*

*professional scrounger, a quick-witted type who makes his
way by attaching himself to rich friends such as Sostratus and
by rendering for them, in return for their hospitality, certain
favors, often of a shady nature. Sostratus has just finished
telling him something as they enter.*)

CHAEREAS   What's this you tell me, Sostratus? You
saw a respectable girl praying to the nymphs here (*gesturing toward the grotto*), and after one look you came away
in love with her?

SOSTRATUS   One look.

CHAEREAS   (*smiling superciliously*)   Pretty quick work.
What did you do? Leave your house with the idea of falling
in love with someone?

SOSTRATUS   (*resentfully*)   It may be a joke to you,
Chaereas, but I'm in a bad way.

CHAEREAS   (*quickly*)   Oh, I believe you.

SOSTRATUS   I consider you not only my friend but a
man who gets things done. That's why I'm bringing you
into this affair.

CHAEREAS   (*with a professional air*)   Well, Sostratus,
here's how I handle affairs of this sort. If a friend of mine
falls in love with some chorus girl and comes to me for
help, I go right out and grab the girl to haul her off to
him; I get drunk, I burn down her door, I don't listen to
reason. The trick is to let him get her before you even find
out her name. Because, if there's any delay, he'll get more
and more infatuated, but if it's done quickly there's a
chance he'll get over it quickly. On the other hand, if a
friend brings up the subject of marriage with a respectable girl, then I'm totally different. I find out the family
background, the family income, what her character is like.
(*With a self-satisfied smile*) You see, I leave my friend
what I arrange as a memorial for the rest of his days.

SOSTRATUS   That sounds fine. (*Aside*)   But not exactly
to my taste.

CHAEREAS   (*rubbing his hands energetically with the
air of a man ready to get right to work*)   Well, now, the
first thing we have to do is hear all about it.

SOSTRATUS   I had Pyrrhias, the servant who went hunting with me, leave the house at the crack of dawn this morning.

CHAEREAS   What for?

SOSTRATUS   To speak to the girl's father or the head of the household, whoever he is.

CHAEREAS   (*disgusted*)   Oh, my god, what's this you're telling me?

SOSTRATUS   (*unhappily*)   I made a mistake. I guess I shouldn't have used a servant for this sort of thing. But when a man's in love, it's hard for him to know what's the right thing to do. (*Looking around anxiously*) I've been wondering for some time now what's been keeping him. I told him to come right back to me as soon as he had found out the lie of the land.

(*At this moment Pyrrhias bursts in, stage right, running at top speed and shouting.*)

PYRRHIAS   Gangway, everybody clear the road! Watch out, there's a lunatic after me, a raving lunatic!

SOSTRATUS   (*grabbing him and forcibly holding him back*)   Hey, what is this?

PYRRHIAS   (*shouting*)   Run for your lives!

SOSTRATUS   What is it?

PYRRHIAS   He's heaving things at me! Sticks and stones! He's going to kill me!

SOSTRATUS   Heaving things? (*As Pyrrhias struggles to get loose*)   Where are you going, you good-for-nothing?

PYRRHIAS   (*looking around warily and not seeing anyone*)   I guess he stopped chasing me.

SOSTRATUS   You're darned right he did.

PYRRHIAS   But I thought he was.

SOSTRATUS   Now what's this all about?

PYRRHIAS   (*still quaking*)   Please! Let's get out of here.

SOSTRATUS   Where?

PYRRHIAS   (*pointing to Cnemon's house*)   Away from that door. As far as we can get. That house you sent me to—

the devil's own son lives there, a demon, a madman. Damnation! I just about broke every one of my toes stumbling around.

SOSTRATUS   (*to Chaereas, gesturing toward Pyrrhias*)
Is he crazy? Or did he come here and get drunk?

CHAEREAS   (*nodding knowingly*)   Crazy. A clear case.

PYRRHIAS   (*excitedly*)   God, no! May I be struck dead on the spot, Sostratus! (*Looking around fearfully*) But be on your guard! (*Heaving and puffing*) I can hardly talk, I'm so out of breath. Well, I knocked on the door and said I wanted the head of the house. Some old witch came out. From the very spot where I'm standing and talking to you now, she pointed to where he was, on a hill dragging himself around to pick up wild pears—or the fires of hell!

CHAEREAS   (*sarcastically*)   Temper, temper!

PYRRHIAS   (*to Chaereas, coldly*)   My dear man, why not? (*To Sostratus*)   Well, I walked off the road into the field and headed toward him. I wanted to be real friendly and tactful, so I called out while I was still some distance away. "I beg your pardon," I said, "but I've come here to see you. I'm very anxious about a matter that concerns you." He starts right in yelling at me, "You god-forsaken good-for-nothing, what do you mean by trespassing on my property?" and then he picks up a clod and heaves it straight at my face.

CHAEREAS   He can go to the devil!

PYRRHIAS   I just about had time to blink and say "God damn you," when he picks up one of his vine stakes and starts clobbering me with it, hollering, "What business can you have with me, anyway? Can't you tell a public road from private property?"—all at the top of his lungs.

CHAEREAS   (*nodding knowingly*)   One of those crazy hicks, that's what you're talking about.

PYRRHIAS   Well, it ended up with me running and him chasing me about a mile and a half, first all around the hill and then down into the brush here, throwing clods and stones at me. Even his pears, when he didn't have anything better. He's a wild one, all right. Some godforsaken old crank! Please! Let's get out of here!

SOSTRATUS   (*stubbornly*)   You mean be a coward?

PYRRHIAS   (*frantically*) You don't understand. We're in danger. He'll eat us alive!

CHAEREAS   Maybe he had some sort of attack just now. That's why, if you ask me, Sostratus, I'd put off seeing him. Always remember that the best way to get anything done is to pick the psychological moment.

PYRRHIAS   That makes sense.

CHAEREAS   These half-starved hicks have mean tempers. Not just this one, but practically all of them. Tomorrow, first thing, I'll go see him by myself, now that I know where he lives. Right now you go home too and take it easy. Everything will turn out all right. (*Takes his leave, stage left.*)

PYRRHIAS   Let's do that.

SOSTRATUS   (*to Pyrrhias, bitterly, gesturing toward the departing Chaereas*) He's glad he found an excuse. I could see right away he wasn't any too anxious to come along with me, and took a dim view of my going after this marriage. But you! Damn you, damn you to hell, you blockhead!

PYRRHIAS   What'd I do that was wrong, Sostratus?

SOSTRATUS   You stole something when you went on his property. No question about it.

PYRRHIAS   (*blankly*) I stole?

SOSTRATUS   Would anyone have beaten you up if you hadn't done something wrong?

PYRRHIAS   (*happening to look up in the direction of the wings, stage right*) Hey, Here he comes!

SOSTRATUS   He is? I'm going! (*Urgently*) Be a good fellow—you talk to him. I couldn't. When I talk, nobody ever believes me. And what do you say . . . [A line and a half is lost here.] He doesn't exactly look like the friendly type. My god, what a scowl! I'd better get a little further away from his door. Look—no one's with him and he's shouting away. If you ask me, he's a sick man. God in heaven, he scares me! It's the truth, let's face it.

(*Cnemon strides in, stage right, talking at the top of his lungs as he goes along. He's all that we have been led to expect: a sour-tempered old codger, gnarled and bent from a lifetime of work in the fields, and utterly indifferent to his appearance—he is dressed in worn work clothes that are a mass of tatters, and his hair is unkempt. His disposition has obviously not been improved by his recent contretemps with Pyrrhias. At the sight of him, Pyrrhias discreetly moves well to the side.)*

CNEMON   (*haranguing the world at large*)   Wasn't that fellow Perseus the lucky one! For two reasons. First, he had wings so he never had to meet anyone walking around on the ground. Second, he had some sort of gadget to turn anyone who bothered him into stone. I wish I had it right now—I'd fill the place with statues. God almighty, life isn't worth living nowadays! Now people trespass on your property to come and jabber away at you. You think I spend time right along the road? I don't even work that part of the property! I've given it up. Too many people passing by. And now they even chase me up into the hills! (*Gritting his teeth and clenching his fists*) Oh, these crowds, these mobs! (*Noticing Sostratus in front of his house*) My god—now here's someone in front of my door! (*Heads straight for Sostratus.*)

SOSTRATUS   (*sotto voce, to Pyrrhias*)   Is he going to hit *me*?

CNEMON   (*as before*)   A man couldn't find any privacy even if he wanted to hang himself!

SOSTRATUS   (*sotto voce, to Pyrrhias*)   He's got it in for me! (*Visibly braces himself. As Cnemon comes near, in his most courteous manner*) I beg your pardon. I'm waiting for someone here. I had an appointment with him.

CNEMON   (*as before*)   Didn't I tell you? (*To Sostratus*) What did you think this was, anyway, a park? a public square? (*With ponderous sarcasm*) If you want to meet people in front of my door, why don't you be sensible about it? Rearrange everything, install a nice comfortable chair here. Better yet, build yourself a town hall. (*To the world at large*) What I have to put up with! Insolence—that's the curse, if you ask me. (*Charges into his house, slamming the door behind him.*)

SOSTRATUS   (*Shaking his head dubiously*)   If you ask

me, ordinary measures aren't going to help. We've got
to do something drastic. No question about it. (*Brightening*) Why don't I go see Geta, my father's servant? By god,
that's what I'll do. He's got a brain that sizzles, and he
knows his way around. He's the fellow to change the old
grouch's mood, I know it. I have no intention of losing any
time in this project; a lot can happen in one day. (*There's
a noise at Cnemon's door.*) Wait—someone's coming out.

(*The door swings open and Cnemon's daughter comes out.
She is dressed as simply as possible and is carrying a homely
kitchen pot, but somehow her radiant young beauty remains
unimpaired. It has a special quality that sets her off, raises
her above everything about her. The minute she closes the door
and turns to the audience, it is apparent that she is greatly
upset.*)

GIRL   (*to herself*) Oh, dear, this is simply terrible! What
    am I going to do? My old nurse went to draw some water
    and dropped the bucket in the well!
SOSTRATUS   (*transfixed at the sight of the girl, to him-
    self*)   Ye gods! Ye gods in heaven! She's beautiful! She's
    irresistible!
GIRL   (*to herself*)   Papa had given orders when he left
    to heat up some water.
SOSTRATUS   (*to the audience, rapturously*)   Gentlemen,
    what do I do?
GIRL   (*to herself*)   And if he ever finds out about this,
    he'll beat her to within an inch of her life. Oh, dear, I
    don't have much time. (*Turns and starts to walk toward
    the grotto.*) My darling nymphs, I'll take some of your
    water. (*Suddenly stops.*) Oh, there may be some people
    praying inside. I'd be mortified if I disturbed them.
SOSTRATUS   (*recovering his wits, approaches her and
    addresses her in his most gallant manner*)   May I? I'll fill
    it for you and bring it right back.
GIRL   Oh yes, please!
SOSTRATUS   (*as he walks toward the grotto*)   Just a
    lovely country girl—but a lady! O Lord, I feel the pangs
    of love—there's no saving me now!

GIRL   (*starting as she hears the creak of a door opening*)
Oh, dear, someone's coming out. Maybe it's Papa! He'll beat
me if he catches me outside here!

(*It is the door of Gorgias' house, not Cnemon's, that opens
and Davus, Gorgias' servant, comes out. The girl breathes a
sigh of relief. Davus is an old, devoted family retainer who
had once belonged to Gorgias' father. But, like many old men,
he has a tendency to be cranky—and the long years of hard
work he has put in helping the family eke out their bare existence hasn't helped his state of mind.*)

DAVUS   (*talking through the doorway to Myrrhina, Gorgias' mother, inside*)   I'm spending ages around here helping you, while he's out there digging all by himself. I'd
better go to him. (*Turns from the door and starts walking,
muttering to himself.*) Oh, this poverty! Why do we have
to have such a bad case of it? Why does it have to move into
our house and live with us like a permanent guest?

(*Sostratus emerges from the grotto with the pot now full
of water and walks toward the girl.*)

SOSTRATUS   Here you are.
GIRL   (*moving to the doorway of her house*)   Please bring
it here.
DAVUS   (*hearing the voices and noticing the two, to him-
self*)   What's that fellow after, anyway?
SOSTRATUS   (*as the girl enters her house*)   Goodbye.
Take care of your father. (*To himself, in despair*) Oh, my
god, my god!
PYRRHIAS   (*soothingly*)   Stop moaning, Sostratus. It's
going to be all right.
SOSTRATUS   All right? How?
PYRRHIAS   Don't worry. You were going after Geta just
now. Go ahead. Tell him everything that's happened and
bring him back with you. (*The two leave, stage left.*)
DAVUS   (*to himself*)   What the devil's going on here?
I don't like this business of a youngster doing favors for
a girl; it's bad stuff. Cnemon, I hope you rot in hell! You

leave an innocent girl by herself in a deserted place, like a foundling, and do nothing to protect her. This youngster probably got wind of the situation and sneaked in here figuring he had hit the jackpot. Well, I've got to tell her brother about this as soon as I can so that we can arrange to keep an eye on her. Matter of fact, I think I'll go do that right now. (*There's a sound of music and song; he looks toward the wings, stage left.*) Besides, I see one of Pan's congregations coming this way—and they're all a little high. If you ask me, this is no time to get in their way. (*Leaves, stage right.*)

(*A chorus, dressed as worshipers of Pan, comes on and dances an entr'acte.*)

ACT II

(*Davus enters, stage right, followed by a man dressed in work clothes that, although worn, are clean and neat. It is Gorgias, Cnemon's stepson. His mother had taken him from Cnemon's household when he was still a child, and it was the best thing she could have done: he has grown into a sturdy, fine-looking young man; despite his dress, you can see at a glance that he is no ordinary peasant. The hard life he is forced to lead hasn't warped him; he has the intelligence and strength of character to take a philosophical view of his situation.*
Davus has just told him about the intruder and the two have come to see if he's still around.)

GORGIAS   You mean to say you handled the situation that badly, that carelessly?
DAVUS   (*on the defensive*)   What do you mean?
GORGIAS   That fellow, whoever he was, was making advances to the girl. Damn it all, you should have talked to him then and there and told him that we don't want to catch him doing this ever again. What you did was to turn your back on it as if it was none of your business. (*Reflectively*) Davus, I guess a man can't get out of family

obligations. A sister of mine is still my concern. Her father chooses to act like a stranger toward us, but we don't have to copy what that old grouch does. Because, if the girl gets involved in a scandal, the blame's going to fall on me too. Outsiders hear about only what's happened, not who's responsible for it. Let's go see the old fellow.

DAVUS   But, Gorgias, I'm afraid of him. The minute he catches me heading for his door, he'll hang me on the spot.

GORGIAS   (*nodding assent gloomily*) Oh, he's a hard one to reason with, all right. I can see absolutely no way we can force him to behave better, or talk him into changing his ways. He's got the law to stop us from doing anything by force—and that temper of his from accomplishing anything by talk. (*Starts walking off.*)

DAVUS   (*looking toward the wings, stage left*) Wait a second. It wasn't a waste of time after all to come here. I told you he'd come back. There he is.

GORGIAS   (*following Davus' glance*) Is that the fellow you were telling me about? With the fancy jacket?

DAVUS   That's the one.

GORGIAS   From the look in his eye you can see right away he's up to no good.

(*Sostratus enters, stage left, so absorbed in his thoughts that he doesn't notice Davus and Gorgias.*)

SOSTRATUS   (*to the audience*) I couldn't get Geta. He wasn't in. My mother's giving a party to celebrate some religious holiday. Don't ask me which—she goes in for this sort of thing every day of the week; goes around the whole town saying prayers. She'd sent him out to hire a cook. I said No, thank you, to the party and came back here. I think I'll quit beating around the bush and speak for myself. (*Walking toward Cnemon's door*) And I'm going to knock on the door right now so's not to give myself time for second thoughts.

GORGIAS   (*coming forward*) Mister, would you mind listening to me for a moment? I've got something important to tell you.

SOSTRATUS   (*looking up in surprise, but responding with*

the courtesy that comes naturally to him) I'd be very glad to. What is it?

GORGIAS (*eyeing Sostratus closely and speaking earnestly and with conviction*) Some of us are well off and some not. But I'm convinced there isn't a man in this world whose situation is permanent; there's always a chance it can change. If a man's well off, things in life will keep going well for him only so long as he's able to handle his good luck and keep from doing wrong. When it comes to the point where he's led astray by the good things he has, then his life is going to take a turn for the worse. On the other hand, take people who aren't well off. If, in spite of all their handicaps, they can keep from doing wrong and can bear up under their fate like men of character, when with time they've won a good name, they can look forward to a better share in life. What do I mean by all this? That you, no matter how well-to-do you are, shouldn't take this state of affairs for granted. Nor should you look down on us just because we're poor. Show the world by your conduct that you deserve your good luck.

SOSTRATUS (*puzzled, not catching the drift of these remarks*) And just what do I seem to you to be doing now that isn't as it should be?

GORGIAS (*looking him straight in the eye*) I think you've been trying hard to do something mean and unworthy. You've got it in mind to talk a respectable girl into doing wrong. You're looking for a chance to do something you ought to pay for with your life.

SOSTRATUS (*stunned*) Oh, my god!

GORGIAS (*taken aback by Sostratus' reaction*) Anyway, you have no right to spend your leisure time hurting people who don't know what leisure is. Remember, there's no one more bitter than a poor man who's been wronged. He's someone you should feel sorry for, to begin with; and, on top of that, in his mind what you do to him is no ordinary wrong but a deliberate insult.

SOSTRATUS (*finally realizing what lies behind all this, earnestly*) Mister, I'm ready to wish you all the luck, wealth, and leisure in the world if you'll just listen to me for a moment.

DAVUS   (*to Gorgias*)   Good work Gorgias! So help me,
that's telling him.

SOSTRATUS   (*to Davus, angrily*)   And you listen too,
blabbermouth! (*To Gorgias*) I saw a girl here. I fell in
love with her. If this is wrong, then I guess I've done a
wrong. What else can a person say? I haven't come here
to make advances to her. I want to see her father. Look,
I'm a respectable Athenian citizen, I've got a good income,
and I'm ready to take her without any dowry and give you
my oath that I'll never stop loving her. (*With deep conviction*) Mister, may this god (*gesturing toward the grotto*)
strike me dead on this spot if I came here to harm or try
some trick on you people behind your back. Believe me,
I'm upset, terribly so, if I've given that sort of impression
to you.

GORGIAS   (*visibly impressed*)   And if I've used stronger
language with you than necessary, please don't feel hurt
any longer. You've not only convinced me, but I'm ready
to be your friend. And, my dear fellow, I'm no stranger
to her. I'm her half-brother; she and I have the same
mother. That's why I'm talking this way to you.

SOSTRATUS   (*excitedly*)   Then you can help me, I
swear, in what comes next.

GORGIAS   (*puzzled*)   Help you?

SOSTRATUS   I can see that you're a gentleman.

GORGIAS   (*shaking his head sadly*)   I don't want to
make up any excuses to get you away from here. I just
want to make clear what the facts of the situation are.
This girl's father is in a class by himself. There's no one
like him alive today, and there never has been.

SOSTRATUS   The old grouch? (*Grimly*)   I know a little
about him.

GORGIAS   They don't come any worse. This property he's
got is worth sixty thousand dollars. He always works it all
by himself. Never gets anybody to help him, no slaves,
no local hired hands, no neighbors. Does it all by himself.
You see, his greatest pleasure in life is not to have to set
eyes on another soul. He usually works with the girl at
his side. She's the only one he'll talk to. As a matter of

fact, he'd find it hard to exchange a word with anyone else. And he claims he won't let her marry until he can find a son-in-law exactly like himself.

SOSTRATUS   You mean never!

GORGIAS   (*urgently*)   My dear fellow, don't go looking for trouble. You'll just be wasting your time. Leave it to us to put up with the situation. We're his relatives; it's our lot in life.

SOSTRATUS   (*heatedly*)   For god's sake, mister, haven't you ever been in love?

GORGIAS   (*gloomily*)   My dear fellow, that's out of the question.

SOSTRATUS   Why? What's to stop you?

GORGIAS   The sum total of all the troubles I'm up against. They don't give me a moment's respite.

SOSTRATUS   (*smiling*)   No, I don't think you ever have been in love. You certainly have a naive way of talking about it. You're asking me to give up. (*Fervently*) That's no longer in my power, only in god's.

GORGIAS   It's not that you're doing us any harm, it's just that you're giving yourself a lot of trouble for nothing.

SOSTRATUS   Can't I get the girl somehow?

GORGIAS   No, you can't. Just come along with me and you'll see; he's working in the valley right near where I am.

SOSTRATUS   How?

GORGIAS   I'll make a remark about getting the girl married; matter of fact, for my part I'd gladly see it happen. He'll wade right in and attack everybody in creation, sneering at the lives they lead. And, if he gets a look at you, the picture of a gentleman of leisure, he won't be able to bear the sight of you.

SOSTRATUS   Is he out there now?

GORGIAS   Oh, no. But he'll go out a little later by the route he usually takes.

SOSTRATUS   (*eagerly*)   And you say he'll have the girl with him?

GORGIAS   It depends. Maybe.

SOSTRATUS   (*resolutely*)   Then I'm ready to go to that place you mentioned. And, please, you've got to help me!

GORGIAS   How?

SOSTRATUS   What do you mean how? Take me to that place you mentioned!

DAVUS   (*eyeing Sostratus coldly*)   What? You plan to stand around in that fancy jacket while we work?

SOSTRATUS   (*ingenuously*)   Certainly. Why not?

DAVUS   He'll start right in heaving rocks at you and calling you a lazy nuisance. No, you're going to have to dig right along with us. That way, if he happens to see you, he'll think you're a poor man who has to work for a living, and he may let you exchange a word with him.

SOSTRATUS   (*enthusiastically*)   Let's go! I'm ready to do whatever you say.

GORGIAS   (*sotto voce, to Davus*)   Why should you force him to suffer?

DAVUS   (*sotto voce, to Gorgias, snarling*)   What I want is to put in a full day's work today—and for him to throw his back out. Then he'll stop coming around and bothering us.

SOSTRATUS   Give me a mattock.

DAVUS   Here, take mine. I'll be working on the fence for a while. That's a job that also has to be done.

SOSTRATUS   Let's have it.   (*As he takes the mattock, feelingly*)   You've saved my life!

DAVUS   (*unable to take any more of this*)   I'll go along; you two follow me there. (*Goes out, stage right.*)

SOSTRATUS   Here's the way I feel: if I get the girl, I'll live; if not, I'll kill myself on the spot.

GORGIAS   If you really mean what you say, I hope you get her. (*Follows Davus out.*)

SOSTRATUS   (*to himself, looking at Gorgias' departing figure*)   Ye gods! The very things you thought would stop me have made me twice as keen to go ahead. The girl's been brought up without any women around her. There's been no aunt or nurse to give her wrong ideas; she doesn't know a thing about the bad side of life. She's had a decent upbringing by a wild-eyed, absolutely strait-laced father. What a blessing to get a girl like that! (*Puts on the work clothes, shoulders the mattock, takes a few steps, then stops.*) This here mattock weighs a ton! It'll kill me! Oh, well, I can't weaken, now that I've started to sweat this business out. (*Hurries out, stage right, to catch up with Davus and Gorgias.*)

(*A second later a man in a cook's outfit enters, stage left, pulling mightily on a rope, on the other end of which is a sheep that is pulling mightily in the opposite direction. The man is Sicon, the chef—or rather, chef and caterer—whom Sostratus' mother had sent Geta out to hire for her party. Sicon has no small opinion of himself and the importance of his profession. But if long on self-esteem, he's a bit short on brains.*)

SICON   (*to himself*)   This is some sheep! No ordinary animal, not this one. (*To the sheep*) Go to the devil! (*To himself*) If I pick it up and carry it, it gets a branch in its teeth, starts eating the leaves, and pulls away from me with all its might. If I put it down to walk, it won't go ahead. Things are reversed—here am I, the one supposed to do the cutting, getting all cut up towing this thing along the road! Thank god, here's the cave where we're going to sacrifice it. Pan, am I glad to see you! (*Looking back in the direction he had come from*) Geta! Look how far behind you are!

(*Geta, Sostratus' father's valet, enters. Geta is a young, agile, resourceful chap—but at this juncture he is in no position to display any of his talents, for he's bent double under a towering load of straw mats.*)

GETA   Those damn women piled enough on me to load four donkeys!
SICON   It looks as if a big crowd's expected. I can't even count all the mats you've got there.
GETA   What do I do with them?
SICON   (*pointing*)   Stack them here.
GETA   (*dumping his load*)   Here you are. (*Grumbling to himself as he straightens up painfully*) All she has to

do is see the Pan from the shrine on the other side of town
in a dream, and I know just what happens: out we march
the next minute to sacrifice to him.

SICON   (*overhearing and, being a highly superstitious
sort, pricking up his ears*)   Who had a dream?

GETA   (*still put out because of the job that had been
given him and in no mood for conversation, particularly
Sicon's*) Oh, don't bother me.

SICON   (*too obtuse to take offense*)   But tell me, Geta,
who had a dream?

GETA   (*curtly*)   My lady.

SICON   (*on tenterhooks*)   What about? For god's sake,
tell me!

GETA   (*disgusted*)   You'll be the death of me. She
thought she saw Pan—

SICON   (*interrupting, pointing to the grotto*)   You mean
the one from here?

GETA   (*patiently*)   The one from here.

SICON   Do what?

GETA   (*continuing*)   —take her son Sostratus—

SICON   (*interrupting again, with a knowing nod*)   A
fine young fellow.

GETA   (*doggedly determined to end his sentence*)   —clap
him in irons—

SICON   Oh, my god!

GETA   —give him some work clothes and a mattock, and
order him to go digging in this field alongside here.

SICON   Amazing!

GETA   That's why we're making this sacrifice. It's an
evil omen. We want to turn it into a good one.

SICON   (*awed*)   Now I understand.   (*Galvanized into action by what he's just heard*)   All right, pick up the mats
again and bring them inside. Let's get the seats set up in
there and everything else all ready. I don't want anything to
hold up the sacrifice when they come, knock on wood.
(*Noticing that Geta is standing there eyeing the stack
of mats darkly, jovially*)   Wipe the frown off! You old
good-for-nothing, I'll tie the feed bag on you today for
real! All the food you want.

GETA   (*giving him a fishy stare*)   I've always had a

good word to say for you and your cooking—but I don't believe you, just the same.

(*Geta picks up his load of mats and the two enter the cave. The stage is now empty, and the chorus re-appears to dance an entr'acte.*)

ACT III

(*The door of Cnemon's house opens and Cnemon comes out. He calls to Simike inside, the ancient female who is his only servant.*)

CNEMON   (*through the doorway*)   Simike! Lock the door and don't open up for anyone until I get back. And that probably won't be until after dark.

(*Cnemon turns from the door and is about to trudge out to his fields when he catches sight of Geta emerging from the cave. Geta walks forward and stands looking toward the wings, stage left, as if he were expecting someone. Suddenly a young servant girl enters, with a number of others behind her.*)

GETA   (*shouting to the girl*)   Plangon! Get a move on! We should have been done with the sacrifice by now!
CNEMON   (*aghast as he eyes the procession straggling in*)   What the devil does this mean? A crowd! Oh, damn them!
GETA   (*to one of the girls who is carrying a flute*)   Parthenis, some of Pan's music! No silent processions for this god, that's what they say.

(*By this time there is a whole group on stage, mostly girls plus a few men. They are Sostratus' mother's servants, and they are carrying all the paraphernalia needed for a sacrifice and a party: incense burner, holy cakes, holy water, kitchenware, tableware, and so on. Sostratus' mother herself is in the crowd. At this point Sicon comes out of the cave,*) *takes one look at the group, and hurries forward to take over.*)

SICON   (*roaring at the servants*)   So you finally make it! Good god, this is disgusting! We've been sitting around here waiting all this time. We got everything we could all ready.

GETA   (*joining in*)   At least the sheep is. I'll swear to that. The poor thing's practically dead. It's not going to hang around while all of you take it easy. Come on now, inside, all of you! (*As they start to file into the cave*) Get everything all set, the baskets, the holy water, the cakes! (To a final straggler) Hey, you! Dumbbell! What are you gaping at? (*Hustles him inside. Cnemon is now alone on the stage.*)

CNEMON   (*shaking his fist at the figures disappearing into the cave*)   God damn you! (*To himself*) They're going to keep me from my work. I can't go off now and leave the house alone. (*Savagely*)   These nymphs—they're a blamed nuisance to have as neighbors the rest of my life. My mind's made up: I'll tear my house down and move somewhere else. (*Gesturing toward the group in the cave*) They sacrifice like a bunch of thieves. They bring couches and jugs of wine—but not for the service. Oh no, it's for themselves. Incense and a holy cake—*that's* an offering, all going to the god right on the altar fire. But these people! *They* must offer an animal—but god gets only the tail and gall bladder, which no one will eat; everything else they gobble up themselves. (*Pounding on his door*) Simike! Hurry and open the door! (*To himself, worriedly*) I guess I'll have to keep an eye on things inside.

(*The door is opened and Cnemon goes inside. A second later Geta comes out of the cave. His first words are addressed to one of the servants inside.*)

GETA   (*shouting through the entrance of the cave*)   You say you forgot to bring the pot? Still sleeping it off, you drunks! What are we going to do now? (*Leaves the entrance and makes his way toward Cnemon's door, grumb-*

ling to himself.) It looks like I'll have to bother one of the god's neighbors. (*Knocks on the door and shouts*) Boy! (*Continues his chain of complaints, punctuating it with shouts to rouse someone within.*) God in heaven, if you ask me they don't grow them worse than that bunch of girls, anywhere. Boy! All they know how to do is get laid—Boy! Please!—and make nasty insinuations about you if you catch them at it. Boy! What the devil is this? Boy! No one home? Ah—it sounds as if someone's running up now.

(*The door opens and Cnemon comes out.*)

CNEMON   (*raging*) Damn you, what are you putting your filthy hands on this door for? Speak up!

GETA   (*taken aback*) Well, you don't have to bite my head off!

CNEMON   By god, I'll eat you alive. (*Takes a threatening step toward him.*)

GETA   (*beating a hasty retreat*) None of that, for god's sake!

CNEMON   (*caustically*) Who are you, one of my creditors, you god-forsaken good-for-nothing!

GETA   (*from a safe distance*) I'm no creditor. Look, I didn't come here to collect a debt. I don't have the sheriff with me. I just came to ask you for a pot.

CNEMON   (*taken aback*) A pot?

GETA   A pot.

CNEMON   (*snarling*) Damn you, what do you think? That I sacrifice oxen whole and carry on the way you people do?

GETA   (*aside*) If you want my opinion, you wouldn't sacrifice a snail. (*To Cnemon*) I'll say good-bye then, sir. The servants told me to knock on the door and ask for a pot. I did. You don't have one. I'll go back and tell them. (*To himself, as he walks away*) Ye gods! That old man's got fangs! (*Enters the cave.*)

CNEMON   (*balefully watching Geta go off*) A bunch of wild animals! Come right up to your door and knock as if you were their best friend. (*Shaking his fist at the cave*) If I catch any of you coming to this door, and if I don't

make an example of him for everyone around here, you can
take it for granted—(*pauses a second, then comes up with
what to him is a terrible indictment*) that I'm just another
of the common herd! (*Turning to go inside*) I don't know
why I let that one off so easy. He was lucky, whoever he
was! (*Enters his house.*)

(*A second later Sicon comes out of the cave. His first words
are addressed to Geta inside.*)

SICON   (*through the entrance of the cave, disgustedly*)
Damn you! He swore at you, you say? Maybe you asked
him the way some dumb hayseed would. (*Grumbling to himself as he walks toward Cnemon's door*) Some people just
don't understand how to do things like this. I'm an expert
at it. I've got thousands of customers back in the city, and
I pester their neighbors and borrow stuff from all of them.
When you borrow from somebody you've got to use a little
flattery. If some old gent answers the door, the first thing
I do is call him "My dear sir"; if it's an old woman, I call
her "Lady"; if it's a middle-aged woman, I call her
"Madame"; if it's a servant, "My good man" or "My dear
boy." You ought to be hung, all of you! What stupidity!
To say (*mimicking Geta's voice*) "Boy, boys"! Here's my
way. (*Knocking on the door*) My dear sir, would you mind
coming out? I'd like to speak to you.
CNEMON   (*as he opens the door*)   You back again?
SICON   (*startled*)   Hey! What's this?
CNEMON   (*eyeing him balefully*)   Are you deliberately try-
ing to make me lose my temper? Didn't I tell you to keep
away from this door? (*Turning and calling inside*) Simike!
Bring me the whip!
SICON   (*as Cnemon grabs him*)   No, no! Let go, let go of
me! Please, for god's sake! (*He breaks loose and races
away.*)
CNEMON   (*raging mad*)   Come back here, you!
SICON   (*forgetting his principles*)   Well, god damn you—
CNEMON   Still jabbering, eh?
SICON   (*getting control of himself again and stopping a*

safe distance away, resentfully) I only came here to ask you for a stew pot.

CNEMON   I don't have a stew pot, and I don't have a cleaver, and I don't have salt or vinegar or anything else. I've told everybody in the neighborhood, in plain language, not to come near me.

SICON   You didn't tell me.

CNEMON   I'm telling you now.

SICON   (*aside*) Yes, and I hope you choke. (*To Cnemon*) Please, couldn't you just tell me where I could borrow one?

CNEMON   (*to the world at large*) What did I tell you? (*To Sicon*) Are you going to keep on jabbering at me?

SICON   Well, thanks anyway.

CNEMON   I don't want any thanks from any of you.

SICON   All right then, no thanks.

CNEMON   (*as he turns to go inside, to himself*) What I have to put up with! And nothing I can do about it.

SICON   (*to himself*) He just about tore me to pieces! That's what you get for asking like a gentleman! (*Ruefully*) It sure makes a difference, doesn't it? What about trying some other door? But it's not going to be easy if everyone in this place is so ready to climb into the ring with you. (*Thinking a moment*) I think the best thing would be to broil all the meat. At least I've got a broiling pan. (*Addressing, as it were, the whole district*) People of Phyle— GOODBYE! (*To himself again*) I'll just make do with what I have. (*Enters the cave.*)

(*Enter Sostratus, stage right. He looks all in: he is covered with dirt, sweat is streaming off him, his hair is disheveled, and he limps along holding his back.*)

SOSTRATUS   (*to himself*) If anyone's running short of trouble, the thing for him to do is go hunting in Phyle. Oh my aching back! And spine, and neck—why go into details? My whole body! (*Pauses and shakes his head mournfully.*) I'm sort of a strong young fellow, so I pitched right in, lifting the mattock way up, the way an old hand would. I pegged away happily—but not for very long. Then

I kept turning around to see whether the old man was coming with the girl. Next thing, damn it all, I'm feeling my back, without letting anyone see me. When the work dragged on and on, I began to bend backward. Gradually I got stiff as a board. Not a soul came along. And the sun began to roast me. There I was, barely able to straighten up each time and then going right down again fast with my whole body, like the boom on a crane, when Gorgias took a look at me and said, "Well, I don't think he's going to come today." "What should we do then?" I shot right back at him. "Let's knock off for the present. We'll look for him tomorrow," he said. Davus was there and he relieved me at the mattock. Well, that's the way the first round went. Then I came back here, god knows I can't tell why. Things just automatically draw me to this place.

(*Geta appears at the mouth of the cave. His first words are to Sicon inside.*)

GETA   (*through the entrance of the cave, exasperated*) What the devil is this? Man dear, you think I've got sixty hands? I light the fire for you, follow you around, carry the cakes, cut the guts, make the dough, serve these things, keep an eye on that fellow, all at the same time—and here am I half blind from the smoke in there! (*Turns from the mouth of the cave rubbing his eyes*) If you ask me, I'm doing nothing but run this affair for them!

SOSTRATUS   (*delighted to see him*)   Hey, Geta!

GETA   (*still rubbing his eyes, grumpily*)   Who wants me?

SOSTRATUS   I do.

GETA   (*not recognizing Sostratus in his bedraggled state*) And who are you?

SOSTRATUS   Don't you see me?

GETA   (*finally recognizing him and, knowing it means more work, not exactly overjoyed*)   I see you. Sostratus.

SOSTRATUS   Tell me, what are you doing here?

GETA   What do you think? We've just finished with the sacrifice, and now we're getting dinner ready for you people.

SOSTRATUS   My mother inside?

GETA   Came a long time ago.

SOSTRATUS   And my father?

GETA   We're expecting him. But you go on in.

SOSTRATUS   First I've got a little errand to do. (*To himself*) In some ways this sacrifice here didn't come at a bad time at all. I'll go right now, just as I am, and invite Gorgias and Davus. Once they've joined in the festivities, they'll be of even more use as allies in getting me my bride.

GETA   (*overhearing*)   What! You're going to go out and invite more people to dinner! (*Changes his attitude abruptly and shrugs his shoulders.*) So far as I'm concerned there can be three thousand of you. I knew all along I wasn't going to get even a taste of anything. Perish the thought! Go on, invite the whole world. After all, you people just slaughtered a fine sheep, a beauty, really something to see. (*Gesturing toward the servants in the cave, sarcastically*) But those women—they're so charming—would they share anything with me? God, no! Not even a pinch of salt!

SOSTRATUS   (*having had a moment, during Geta's grumblings, to think his plan over and more pleased than ever with it*)   Geta, before this day is over everything's going to be all right. (*Turning toward the grotto, ebulliently*) Pan, this is one prophecy I'll take it on myself to make. (*Suddenly aware of his presumption, deferentially*) But I'll have a prayer for you every time I pass this way and I'll always treat you with every respect. (*Goes off, stage right, to get Gorgias and Davus.*)

(*The door of Cnemon's house flies open and Simike, Cnemon's aged servant, bursts out. She is in a state of alarm that borders on the pathological.*)

SIMIKE   (*screaming*)   I'm done for! It's all over! This is the end!

GETA   (*stopped by the noise just as he was about to enter the cave*)   Oh, go to the devil! Some woman's come out of the old man's house.

SIMIKE   (*recovering somewhat, to herself*)   What's go-

ing to happen to me? I wanted to see if I could get the
bucket out of the well myself before Cnemon found out, so
I tied his hoe to a rope. Well, it wasn't strong enough, and
it was rotten anyway, and suddenly it broke.

GETA   (*aside*) Good!

SIMIKE   (*to herself*) So now, heaven help me, I've
dropped the hoe down the well along with the bucket!

GETA   (*aside*) Only thing left is to throw yourself in
too.

SIMIKE   (*to herself*) And it *would* happen just now,
when he wants to shift some manure that's in the yard.
He's been running around for ages looking for the hoe,
yelling bloody murder—(*hearing a noise at the door, starts*)
and now he's coming out here!

GETA   (*to Simike*) Run! Run for your life! Woman,
he'll slaughter you! (*Seeing Cnemon coming out*) Too late.
Better protect yourself!

CNEMON   (*roaring*) Where's that thief?

SIMIKE   (*terrified*) Please! I didn't mean to do it!

CNEMON   (*savagely*) Get inside!

SIMIKE   (*as before*) Please! Please! What are you going
to do?

CNEMON   Do? I'm going to tie you to a rope and lower
you down the well myself.

SIMIKE   (*shrieking*) No! Oh, this is terrible!

GETA   (*aside*) Best thing, I swear, is to use the same
rope—if it's really rotten through and through.

SIMIKE   (*in despair, to herself*) I'll call Davus from
next door.

CNEMON   Call Davus? How dare you talk like that, you
old witch! Are you deaf? Get inside! Quick! (*Simike rushes
inside. To himself, exasperated*) Oh lord help me! Oh lord,
here am I all alone! Oh lord, nobody could be worse off!
(*Shrugging*) I'll go down the well myself. What else is
there to do?

GETA   (*overhearing him, maliciously*) We'll be glad to
give you a rope.

CNEMON   (*turning on him*) Before you give me anything you can go fry in hell!

GETA   (*aside*) And I'd deserve to! (*As Cnemon stalks

into his house) He's galloped inside again. Poor devil, what a life he leads! Perfect example of the typical Athenian peasant: becomes an expert in hardship, fighting it out with the rocks around here that grow nothing better than thyme and sage, and getting nothing good out of it. (*Stands silent for a moment pondering this. Then, hearing a noise, looks toward the wings, stage right.*) Here comes Sostratus. And he's got his guests with him. (*Looks again, not believing his eyes.*) They're some of the local farm hands! What a crazy idea! What's he bringing them here for? Where did he get to know them anyway?

(*Sostratus, Gorgias and Davus enter, stage right. Sostratus has issued his invitation and Gorgias has obviously been trying to beg off.*)

SOSTRATUS   (*emphatically*)   I won't hear of your doing otherwise. (*Mimicking Gorgias*) "No, thank you." God almighty, there isn't a man alive who can refuse to come to dinner when his friend's made a sacrifice and is holding a party! And remember, I've been a friend of yours a long time, even before I ever saw you. (*To Davus*) Take your things inside and then come right back.

GORGIAS   I can't leave my mother alone in the house.

SOSTRATUS   Well, take care of whatever she needs. I'll be right back here myself.

(*Sostratus goes into the cave, and Gorgias, with Davus at his heels, into his house. The stage is now clear, and the chorus comes on and dances an entr'acte.*)

ACT IV

(*The door of Cnemon's house is flung open and Simike bursts out, wild-eyed and screaming at the top of her lungs.*)

SIMIKE   Please help! Oh, my god, someone please help!

(*Sicon, attracted by the noise, emerges from the grotto.*)

SICON   (*grumbling*)   In the name of all that's holy, can't you people let us carry on a service in peace! You insult us, you hit us, you scream—what a crazy household!

SIMIKE   (*running up to him*)   My master! He fell into the well!

SICON   How?

SIMIKE   How? He started to go down to get the hoe and the bucket, and he slipped and fell all the way to the bottom.

SICON   (*a broad grin spreading over his face*)   Not the old grouch? By god, it couldn't have happened to a better man! Old lady, you've got a job now.

SIMIKE   What?

SICON   Pick up a boulder or a big rock or something like that and drop it in on top of him.

SIMIKE   (*too distraught to resent Sicon's attitude*) Please! Go down after him!

SICON   What? And become like that fellow in Aesop's fable and have to fight a dog in a well? Not on your life!

SIMIKE   (*leaving him and running toward Gorgias' house*)   Gorgias! Where in the world are you!

GORGIAS   (*as he comes out of his house*)   Here I am. (*Seeing the old woman*) Simike! What's the matter?

SIMIKE   (*impatiently*)   The matter? I'll tell it all over again: Cnemon fell into the well.

GORGIAS   (*galvanized into action, rushes to the entrance of the grotto*)   Sostratus! Come on out here! (*As Sostratus dashes out of the cave, Gorgias turns to Simike.*) Show us the way! Come on, inside now! Quick! (*The three rush into Cnemon's house.*)

SICON   (*watches them go in, then turns and addresses the audience with an air of great satisfaction*)   I'll be damned! Now I believe in Providence. Cnemon, you cheapskate, so you won't lend people a measly pot for a sacrifice, you have to begrudge it, eh? Now that you're down there, drink the well dry so you won't have to share the water with anyone. These nymphs here have taken a hand and given me my revenge—and it's just what you deserve. (*Puffing out his chest*) No one ever harmed a cook yet and got away with it. There's something sacred about our profession. A

waiter's a different matter; you can do what you want to a
waiter. (*Yielding to curiosity, walks over to Cnemon's door
and puts his ear to it.*) He's not dead, is he? Somebody's
crying and moaning, "Papa dear!". [Four lines are lost
here in which Sicon very likely relayed to the audience
whatever he could pick up about the way the rescue was
going] . . . that way they'll be able to haul him out. (*Grinning*) Lord in heaven, can you imagine what a sight it's
going to be—the old man soaked to the skin, shivering
away? Delicious, I'd say. Gentlemen, so help me, nothing
would give me greater pleasure than to see it. (*Walking
to the cave and shouting into it*) You women in there! Let's
hold a service for the rescue party. And say a prayer for
the old man to be saved—provided he's left good and lame,
a cripple. That way there'll be no trouble whatsoever from
him even though he is the god's next-door neighbor and
around here whenever anyone comes to sacrifice. This will
mean a lot to me the next time someone hires me. (*Enters
the cave.*)

(*The door of Cnemon's house flies open and Sostratus comes
running out.*)

SOSTRATUS   (*flushed and in a state of great excitement,
to the audience*)   Gentlemen! I swear to you, on my honor,
by heaven, by all that's holy, I never in my whole life saw
anyone pick a better moment to miss drowning by a hair.
What a marvelous time I had! The minute we got inside
there, Gorgias jumped into the well. The girl and I just
waited around the rim. What else was there to do? Except
that she kept tearing her hair and beating her breast and
crying her eyes out and I, (*archly*) the fine fair-haired
boy, stood by and played nursemaid. I kept begging and
pleading with her not to carry on so, and all the time I
just couldn't take my eyes off her. She's a work of art!
And no ordinary one either. I forgot all about the old man
groaning down there—except that it was a real nuisance
to have to keep hauling away at him all the time. As a
matter of fact, I nearly sent him to his grave: I was so
busy looking at the girl that I let go of the rope a couple

of times. But that Gorgias is an Atlas—and no ordinary
one either; he managed to hang on and finally fished him
out. As soon as the old man was safe, I had to come out
here. I just couldn't hold myself in any longer. I practically went up to the girl and kissed her—that's how
madly in love with her I am. I'm getting ready—wait;
they're coming out. (*Cnemon's door opens, and Cnemon,
supported by Gorgias and flanked by his daughter, comes
hobbling out.*) My god! There's a sight for you! (*Moves off
to the side, out of their range of vision.*)

(*Slowly Cnemon, Gorgias, and the girl make their way
from the door to stage center. There they stand, the girl mute
and terrified, and the old man kept from collapsing by his
stepson's arm.*)

GORGIAS   (*with great solicitude*)   Cnemon! Tell me, is
there anything you want?
CNEMON   (*weakly*)   What can I want? I'm a terribly
sick man.
GORGIAS   Come on now, buck up!
CNEMON   (*dully*)   I'm done bucking up. I'm not going
to bother you any more for the rest of time.
GORGIAS   That's what it is to cut yourself off from every-
body. You see? You almost lost your life just now! At your
age you've got to have someone keep an eye on you as long
as you live.
CNEMON   (*weakly*)   I'm in a bad way. I know it.
Gorgias, go call your mother.
GORGIAS   Of course. Right away. (*To himself, as he goes
into his house*) It certainly looks as if the only way we
learn is by bitter experience.
CNEMON   (*to the girl*)   My dear, will you take my arm
and help hold me up?
SOSTRATUS   (*aside*)   Lucky man!
CNEMON   (*overhearing, turns, sees him—and revives at
the prospect of being irascible again*)   And just what the
devil are *you* standing around here for? [Eight lines are
lost here. After concluding his remarks to Sostratus,
Cnemon turned to his son and daughter and his wife,

Myrrhina, who had come on stage in the meantime, and
continued to unburden his heart, particularly his anguish
at his crippled condition.] None of you could change my
mind about this. (*Holding up his hand as they attempt to
protest*) Don't argue with me. (*Shaking his head ruefully*)
I guess the one mistake I made was in thinking I was the
one person who was completely self-sufficient, who'd never
have need of anyone else. Well, now when I see how strange
and sudden the end of a man's life can be, I realize how
little I knew. A man has to have someone standing by who
can look after him. (*Falls silent a moment, brooding. Then,
passionately*) What ruined me was seeing how everybody
lived, the ways in which they went grubbing after money—
as god's my witness, I was convinced the person didn't exist
who had a kind thought for anybody else. This was what
blinded me. (*Dropping his voice and speaking with deep
feeling*) Only now have I gotten proof, from one man—
Gorgias. He did something that only the finest sort of person would have done. I never let him come near my door,
never helped him in the slightest, never said hello to him,
never exchanged a kind word with him—and yet he saved
my life. Anyone else in his place would have said, and with
good reason: "You never let me near your door, so I'm not
going there now. You never went out of your way for me,
so now I won't for you." (*Seeing Gorgias turn away in
modest embarassment*) What's the matter, my boy? (*Resuming his discourse*) Whether I die now—and I'm convinced I will; I'm in considerable pain—or whether I live,
I'm acknowledging you here and now as my son. Everything I happen to own you are to consider yours. (*Taking
the girl's hand and putting it in Gorgias'*) I put her into
your care. Get her a husband. (*Shaking his head sadly*)
You see, even if conceivably I should get well, *I* couldn't
find one; after all, the man doesn't exist who could satisfy
me. If I survive, just let me go on living the way I want.
Everything else I leave to you to do—you've got good sense,
thank god, and you care for your sister, as you should.
Divide my estate in two. Give her half as a dowry. You
take the other half, run it yourself, and just give your
mother and me enough to live on. (*Turning to the girl*)

Help me, my dear; I want to go in and lie down. I think the sign of a man of good sense is that he doesn't say any more than he has to. (*Continuing right on, to Gorgias*) But there's one thing I want you to know, my boy. I want to say a few words to you about myself and my character. If there were only men like me in this world, we wouldn't have any law courts, people wouldn't drag each other off to prison, there wouldn't be any wars, and we'd all be satisfied with a modest lot in life. But you probably like things the way they are, so you'd better live your life accordingly. (*Wryly*) Besides, you won't have a mean old grouch in your way any longer.

GORGIAS   (*diplomatically*)   Very well. I agree to everything you say. But I insist that you help me find a husband for my sister just as soon as we can—provided you agree.

CNEMON   (*sharply*)   Listen here, I meant every word I said. Now, in god's name, leave me alone!

GORGIAS   You see, there's someone who wants to meet you—

CNEMON   (*interrupting*)   In god's name, no!

GORGIAS   (*stoutly finishing his sentence*)   —and ask your permission to marry her.

CNEMON   (*starting to hobble toward his door*)   It's none of my business from now on.

GORGIAS   (*calling after him*)   He helped save your life.

CNEMON   (*stopping abruptly, interested*)   Who is he?

GORGIAS   (*pointing to Sostratus*)   There he is. (*Beckoning to Sostratus*) Come here.

CNEMON   (*scrutinizing him closely, to Gorgias*)   He's all sunburned. Is he a farmer?

SOSTRATUS   (*quickly*)   Yes, sir!

CNEMON   Not a rich playboy or the kind that wanders around all day doing nothing?

[Five lines are lost at this point. Apparently Cnemon agrees to the match, leaves it to Gorgias to arrange the details, and, supported by his wife and daughter, goes inside to lie down.]

SOSTRATUS   My father won't raise any objections.

GORGIAS   Then, Sostratus, I hereby betroth her to you,

in front of these witnesses, and make over to you the full portion of the estate it's fair for you to get as dowry. You entered into this affair with an honest heart and in all sincerity; and you didn't think it beneath you to do whatevery you could to marry her. Here you are, a man raised in the lap of luxury, and yet you were willing to handle a mattock and dig away and not spare yourself. This is what shows the true man—whether, even though he's rich, he can submit to putting himself on a level with those who are poor. That kind of man will be able to take the ups and downs of life in stride. You've given me enough proof of your character. I only hope you can stay just as you are.

SOSTRATUS   (*swelling under Gorgias' paeans of praise*) I can even do better than that—but, well, this praising oneself isn't exactly the thing to do, you know. (*Turns away in embarrassment and happens to look toward the wings, stage left.*) There's my father! He couldn't have come at a better time.

GORGIAS   (*looking, in surprise*) Is Callippides your father?

SOSTRATUS   Of course.

GORGIAS   Well, by god, he's one rich man who deserves every cent he has. When it comes to running a farm, nothing gets him down.

(*Callippides enters, stage left. He's a portly old fellow, dressed modestly but carefully and in the best of taste. He gives the impression of being affable and good-natured despite the fact that at the moment he's in a foul temper.*)

CALLIPPIDES   (*as he comes on stage, to himself*) I've probably missed everything. They must have picked the bones of that sheep clean by now and all gone off to the farm.

GORGIAS   (*to Sostratus, sotto voce*) My god! He must be starving! Shall we ask him right now?

SOSTRATUS   (*to Gorgias, sotto voce*) Let him eat first. He'll be easier to handle.

CALLIPPIDES   (*seeing Sostratus*) Hey, Sostratus, have you people finished eating?

SOSTRATUS   Yes, but there's some left for you. Go on in.
CALLIPPIDES   That's just what I'm going to do. (*Hurries into the cave.*)
GORGIAS   You go in. That way you can talk to your father in private, if you want.
SOSTRATUS   (*gesturing   towards   Cnemon's   house*) You'll wait for me inside, right?
GORGIAS   I'll stay right there.
SOSTRATUS   I'll call you then in a little while.

(*Sostratus goes into the cave and Gorgias into Cnemon's house. The stage is now empty, and the chorus comes out and dances an entr'acte.*)

ACT V

(*Sostratus and Callippides emerge from the cave. Callippides' disposition has benefited enormously from the meal he has just put away, and the tête-à-tête with his son has, to all appearances, left him unperturbed. Not so Sostratus, who is clearly rather upset.*)

SOSTRATUS   (*unhappily*)   Father, you haven't done everything I wanted—or expected of you.
CALLIPPIDES   (*surprised*)   What's the matter? Didn't I agree with you? I want you to have this girl you're in love with. I say you should marry her.
SOSTRATUS   (*moodily*)   Well, you don't look it.
CALLIPPIDES   So help me, I do want it. Because I know when a young fellow makes up his mind to take the plunge because he's in love, that's a marriage that's bound to last.
SOSTRATUS   So I'm to marry Gorgias' sister, since I consider him just as good as any of us? Then how can you refuse now to let him marry my sister in return?
CALLIPPIDES   (*refusing to take the matter seriously*) Perish the thought! I don't want to acquire two impoverished in-laws. One in the family's enough.

SOSTRATUS   (*refusing to take the matter lightly*)   Ah,
so it's money you're talking about. Now *there's* something
you just can't count on. If you're sure it will stay with
you to the end of your days, then go right ahead, don't
share it with another soul, since you're in charge. But
if it's not yours, if everything you've got you owe to luck,
why begrudge it to others, Father? Lady Luck can always
take every penny away from you and give it in turn to
someone else, maybe someone who doesn't deserve it. That's
why I insist, Father, that, so long as you're in charge, you
be generous with it, help everybody, make life easier for
as many as you can. Such acts never die. If Fate ever deals
you a blow, those you've helped will help you. You know,
it's much better to have a friend you can see before your
eyes than any treasure you keep buried out of sight.
CALLIPPIDES   (*resentfully*)   Sostratus! You know how
it is. I'm not going to take the money I've made to the grave
with me. Anyway, how could I? It's all intended for you.
(*Sighs good-naturedly.*) You want to win yourself a new
friend? Go ahead, since you're sure of him, and good luck
to you. But you don't need to preach sermons to me. Go
on, hand the money out, give it away, share it. You've
convinced me. Absolutely.
SOSTRATUS   (*dubiously*)   You really mean that?
CALLIPPIDES   (*heartily*)   Every word of it, believe
me. Don't you worry your head about that.
SOSTRATUS   (*finally convinced*)   Then I'll call Gorgias.

(*At this moment Gorgias emerges from the door of
Cnemon's house and walks toward them.*)

GORGIAS   (*to the two of them, apologetically*)   I was on
my way out, and, as I came to the door, I couldn't help
overhearing every word you two said. (*To Sostratus*) What
can I say? I consider you a true friend, and I can't tell you
how devoted I am to you. But I don't want a way of life
that's beyond me. God knows I couldn't put up with it
even if I wanted it!
SOSTRATUS   I don't know what you're talking about.

GORGIAS   I'm giving you my sister to marry. But to marry yours—well, thanks, but . . .

SOSTRATUS   What do you mean, "thanks, but"?

GORGIAS   (*blurting out something he has obviously been giving serious thought*)   I don't think I'd enjoy living a life of leisure on money that other people have worked for. A man should earn his own way.

SOSTRATUS   Gorgias! Stop talking nonsense! Don't you think you're good enough for her?

GORGIAS   Oh, I think I'm good enough for her, all right. But I feel it's wrong for a man with a modest portion to accept a large one.

CALLIPPIDES   (*breaking in on the conversation before it gets too far off the ground*)   God in heaven, this is very noble and all that, but you're being silly.

GORGIAS   How so?

CALLIPPIDES   You have no money but you want to act like someone who does. Well, you see I'm convinced . . . [Three fragmentary lines follow in which Callippides talks Gorgias into accepting the match.]

GORGIAS   You win. The only thing left to do is arrange the details.

CALLIPPIDES   (*to Gorgias, solemnly*)   My boy, I hereby betroth my daughter to you to be your lawfully wedded wife. And I'm giving you a dowry of ninety thousand dollars.

GORGIAS   And I have thirty thousand that goes with my sister.

CALLIPPIDES   You have? Now don't overdo it!

GORGIAS   (*stoutly*)   I have plenty.

CALLIPPIDES   (*putting an arm around him, and smiling*)   Keep all that you have, my boy. Now go and bring your mother and sister over here to meet the women in our family.

GORGIAS   All right.

SOSTRATUS   (*enthusiastically*)   Let's all of us spend the night here and have a party. And tomorrow we'll hold a double wedding. Gorgias, bring Cnemon over. He probably stands a better chance of getting the attention he needs with us over here.

GORGIAS   (*gloomily*)   He won't come, Sostratus.

SOSTRATUS   (*as before*)   Talk him into it!

GORGIAS   If I can. (*Turns and goes into Cnemon's house.*)

SOSTRATUS   Father, you know what we ought to do now? Arrange a nice drinking session for us and a get-together for the women.

CALLIPPIDES   (*dryly*)   It'll be just the other way around, believe me: they'll have the nice drinking session, and we'll have the get-together. Well, I'll go ahead and get things ready for you fellows. (*Enters the cave.*)

SOSTRATUS   (*to Callippides as he leaves*)   Do that. (*To himself, musingly*) If a man's got sense he'll never give up, no matter how hopeless a situation is. There isn't anything you can't get—if you care enough and work hard enough for it. I'm the living proof. Not a man alive would have thought this marriage was possible—and yet I brought it off. And in just one day!

(*The door of Cnemon's house opens, and Gorgias comes out followed by his half-sister and his mother.*)

GORGIAS   (*to his mother and sister*)   Come, let's hurry.

SOSTRATUS   (*calling to them*)   Right this way. (*Calling to his mother in the cave*) Mother, would you please make these people welcome? (*As the two women enter the cave, to Gorgias*) Cnemon not here yet?

GORGIAS   Cnemon? He even begged me to take the old woman away so he could be all by himself.

SOSTRATUS   What can you do with a man like that?

GORGIAS   That's the way he is.

SOSTRATUS   (*shrugging*)   I hope he enjoys himself. Let's go in.

GORGIAS   (*holding back*)   I'm terribly embarrassed when there are women around.

SOSTRATUS   (*taking him by the arm and leading him in*)   Don't talk nonsense! Come on in, will you? You've got to remember that it's all in the family now. (*The two enter the cave.*)

(*Cnemon's door opens and Simike comes out. She stops at the threshold to talk to Cnemon inside.*)

SIMIKE   (*through the doorway*)   All right, all right, I'll go too. Lie there all alone. Dear, dear, you're simply impossible! They were nice enough to invite you to the party, but you had to say No. Something dreadful is going to happen to you, I swear, worse than just now.

(*Simike closes the door and starts walking toward the cave. At this moment Geta comes out of the cave and stands at the entrance, talking to the people inside.*)

GETA   (*grumbling at having to leave the party, particularly for such a purpose*)   All right, I'll go and see how he is. (*A mocking trill on the flute is heard from inside.*) Damn you, what are you tootling at me for? I still have things to do. They're sending me to look in on the patient. Cut it out!

SIMIKE   (*overhearing*)   Yes, one of you people should go inside and sit with him. My little girl is leaving me, and I want to have a chat, pay my respects, and say goodbye.

GETA   (*his whole attitude changing as inspiration seizes him, heartily*)   You're absolutely right. You go ahead. I'll take care of him in the meantime. (*Watches Simike enter the cave. As soon as she disappears inside, to himself gleefully*) I've been just waiting for a chance like this. [Geta has two more lines which have been lost. After delivering them he calls through the mouth of the cave.] Sicon! Come on out here! On the double! (*To the world at large*) By god, I think we're going to have *some* fun!

SICON   Were you calling me?

GETA   I certainly was. Listen, do you want to get even for the insults you had to take a little while ago?

SICON   (*in high dudgeon*)   Me? Insulted? What the hell do you mean by that nonsense?

GETA   (*excitedly*)   The old grouch is fast asleep, all alone.

SICON   (*forgetting his dudgeon and interested, but hesitant*)   How's he doing anyway?

GETA   Not too bad.

SICON   (*worriedly*)   Couldn't he get up and hit us?

GETA   He's not going to do any getting up if you ask me.

SICON   (*enthusiastically*)   Those words are music to my ears. I'll go in there and ask to borrow things. That'll drive him out of his mind.

GETA   Wait! What do you say, we first haul him outside and put him down here. Then let's bang on the door and ask to borrow things, and watch his temperature rise. Boy will we have fun!

SICON   (*worried again*)   I'm scared of Gorgias. If he catches us, he'll tan our hides.

GETA   (*gesturing toward the cave*)   Listen to the racket in there. They're getting drunk. Nobody'll hear a thing. (*Grimly*)   It's all up to us. We've *got* to tame this grouch. Don't you see? We're his in-laws, he's one of the family now—and if he keeps on the way he is, what a cross to bear!

SICON   (*nodding assent gloomily*)   You're right.

GETA   The one thing to watch out for is that you don't make any noise when you bring him out here. Come on! (*Geta rushes to Cnemon's door.*)

SICON   (*following*)   Wait a second, please! (*Catching up at the doorway*)   Now don't you run away and leave me. (*Geta shakes his head vigorously to reassure him.*)   And for god's sake, don't make any noise!

GETA   I'm not making a sound, I swear.

(*The two disappear into the house. A second later they emerge, Geta in the lead and Sicon after him, doubled under the weight of Cnemon, still asleep, slung on his back.*)

GETA   (*whispering*)   Over here to the right.

SICON   (*staggering over to the spot where Geta is standing, whispering*)   Here you are.

GETA   (*whispering*)   Put him down here. Now's the time!

(*The two walk stealthily up to the door of Cnemon's house and take their stand there.*)

SICON   (*excitedly*) I'll go first. Ready—you take the beat from me. (*Starts pounding on the door in a regular rhythm and shouting to the imaginary servants inside.*) Boy! Hey, boy! Hey there, boys! Boys! Boys!

CNEMON   (*waking with a start and not yet fully aware of what is happening to him, groaning*) Oh, my god, this is the end of me!

GETA   (*joining Sicon in the measured pounding and shouting*) Hey there, boys! Boy! Hey, boy! Boy! Boys!

Cnemon   My god, it's the end, the end.

GETA   Who's that? (*Turning from the door towards Cnemon*) You from this house?

CNEMON   (*snarling*) Obviously. You—what do you want?

SICON   (*to the imaginary servants inside*) I want to borrow some pots from you people. And a bowl.

CNEMON   (*shouting*) Lift me up, somebody!

SICON   (*ignoring him*) You have some, all right. I know it for sure.

GETA   (*imitating Sicon*) And seven pot stands and twelve tables. (*To imaginary servants outside*) Hey, boys! Tell them inside there what we need. We're in a hurry.

CNEMON   (*snarling*) I don't have a thing.

GETA   You don't, eh?

CNEMON   No, I don't. I told you so a thousand times.

GETA   I'm going then. (*Moves away from the door.*)

CNEMON   (*to himself*) Oh, my god, my god, how did I get out here? Who put me down in front here? (*To Geta*) Yes! Go!

SICON   (*starting the rhythmic pounding all over again*) Here we go. Boy! Hey, boy! Women! Men! Boy! Answer the door!

CNEMON   (*raging*) Are you crazy? You'll break down the door!

SICON   (*to the imaginary servants inside*) Bring us nine rugs.

CNEMON   Where from?

SICON   (*as before*) And an oriental tapestry of embroidered linen, one hundred feet long.

CNEMON   (*in despair*)   If I only had a whip! The old woman—where's the old woman?

SICON   I'll try some other house.

CNEMON   Go right ahead, both of you. (*Shouting frantically*) Simike! Simike! (*To Geta, who is now planted at the door*) God damn you to hell, now what do you want?

GETA   I want a bowl. A big metal bowl.

CNEMON   (*shouting desperately*)   Lift me up, somebody!

SICON   You've got one, all right. And I know you've got the tapestry too, Dad.

CNEMON   God damn it, no! And no bowl. (*Gnashing his teeth*) I'll kill that Simike!

(*Geta at this point signals Sicon to keep quiet, steps forward, and stands over the helpless Cnemon.*)

GETA   (*disgustedly*)   Stop complaining and go back to sleep! (*Speaking slowly and with great emphasis*) You keep away from people. You hate women. You won't let yourself be carried to a friendly party. You're going to put up with every one of those things! There's no one around to help you. (*As Cnemon opens his mouth to talk*) Just shut your face!

SICON   Now, you're going to hear every single thing . . . [Two and a half lines are lost here in which Sicon launched into a description of what was going on in the cave]. Your wife and your daughter got a warm greeting, and they're having a fine time. (*Clearing his throat and making other obvious preparations for an extended harangue*) To go back a little. There I was preparing a party for these gentlemen. (*Indicates by a gesture the men in the cave. Cnemon falls back and closes his eyes wearily.*) You hear me? Don't you fall asleep!

CNEMON   (*helplessly*)   Not fall asleep! Oh, my god!

SICON   (*with mock solicitude*)   What's that? You want to be at the party? You're going to hear me out first. (*Resuming his narrative manner*) There was a great fuss. I laid out the places and set the tables myself. It was my responsibility and I did it. You hear me? (*Striking his chest*) I'm a cook, that's what I am, and don't you forget it!

GETA   (*to the audience, gesturing towards Sicon*)   He's a softie.

(*A burst of music and song and laughter is heard from the cave. Cnemon raises his head wonderingly and Sicon seizes the chance to rub it in.*)

SICON   (*waxing rhapsodic*)   Someone took a fine old wine, poured it into the bosom of a bowl, mixed it with spring water from the cave, and went the rounds inviting the men to have a drink. And someone else did the same for the ladies. But it's like trying to irrigate a desert! You understand that, don't you? And one of the serving girls who got a little high put a veil over her pretty little face and began to dance—but modestly, hesitating and nervous. Then another joined hands and danced with her.

GETA   (*grabbing Cnemon's hand*)   You've been through something terrible. Now join the dance. Come on!

CNEMON   Damn you! What do you want from me, anyway?

GETA   Enough of that. Join the dance. You're being an old hick.

CNEMON   God damn it, no!

GETA   Then we'll carry you in.

CNEMON   (*in despair, to himself*)   What can I do?

GETA   Dance!

CNEMON   All right, carry me in. I'm probably better off putting up with the party in there.

GETA   Now you're talking sense. (*To Sicon and a slave, one of a group that has clustered in the meantime about the entrance to the cave*) Hurray! We've won! Donax and you, Sicon, pick him up and carry him inside. (*To Cnemon*) And you watch yourself; if we catch you making any trouble again, you're not going to get off so easily, believe me. (*Shouting*) Bring us garlands and a torch, someone!

SICON   (*taking a garland from a slave and handing it to Geta*)   Here, take this.

GETA   Good. (*Moving downstage to address the audience*)
If you enjoyed the way we won the fight with this old
troublemaker, let's have a hearty round of applause from
all of you, every boy, youth, and man here!

Any may that maid who loves to laugh, the noble goddess
of victory, be on our side forever!

The Woman of Samos

DRAMATIS PERSONAE

DEMEAS, a well-to-do, elderly citizen of Athens
CHRYSIS, the woman of Samos; a youngish, good-looking
  woman whom Demeas had taken in and made his common-
  law wife
MOSCHION, a young man about town, adopted son of Demeas
NICERATUS, Demeas' neighbor, a poor, elderly citizen of
  Athens
PARMENO, Demeas' valet (slave)
A COOK
[PLANGON, daughter of Niceratus]

SCENE

A street in Athens. Two houses, Demeas' and Niceratus',
front on it. The exit on stage left leads downtown, that on
stage right to the waterfront.

ACT I

(*Moschion comes out of Demeas' house. A youth in his early
twenties, he is expensively dressed, as one would expect of the
only child of a rich father. Though he is handsome, his looks
are not particularly attractive; they give the impression of*

weakness and self-interest. At the moment they give without question the impression that there is something very much on his mind. He moves downstage to unburden himself to the audience.)

[The first fifteen or so lines are lost. The text opens as Moschion turns to the crux of his problem, his father Demeas —actually his foster-father, as we learn later.]

MOSCHION   (*to the audience*)   I think I could easily do this for you by describing what sort of man he is. My recollection of the life of luxury I lived even when I was a child is very clear, but I'll pass over it; it helps not to think of these things any longer. I was duly registered, just like everyone else—one of the crowd, as the saying goes. Now, god knows, I'm worse off than all of them! I made quite a splash when I served my term as patron of the theatre; I made quite a splash in public, since I had horses and dogs that he kept for me; I was a shining light in the guards during my military service; I was able to give a fair amount of help to friends of mine in need. Thanks to him, I was somebody. On the other hand, I showed the proper gratitude to him for all this. I behaved the right way.

Now, it happened that some time after this—I've got nothing to do at the moment, so I'll give you our whole story at once—my father became passionate about some courtesan from Samos, the sort of thing that could happen to any man. He kept it a secret; he was ashamed. In spite of this, I learned about it, and this was the way I figured it: if he doesn't make her his mistress, he'll have competition from young fellows and that will get on his nerves; but maybe, because of me, he's ashamed to take the step . . .

[About twenty-five lines are lost here in which Moschion continues his narrative of the events that led up to his problem. What they were we can deduce from what follows. His father overcame whatever inhibitions he may have had and took the woman from Samos in as his common-law wife. He then went abroad on a long business trip. She was pregnant at the time, and he warned her that, if she had the child while he was away, she was to abandon it, since under the law the issue of a union such as theirs would be illegitimate.

Accompanying Demeas on the trip was his next-door neighbor, Niceratus. Whereas Demeas was quite comfortably off, Niceratus had to make every penny count. His family consisted of his wife and a grown daughter, Plangon, whose future was a particular source of worry to him since he was too poor to afford a dowry.

The text resumes as Moschion describes how neighborly the women in the families became while the two men were away.]

Plangon and her mother were very kind to my father's mistress. She spent lots of time at their house, and they spent lots at ours.

Well, one day when I came hurrying back from our country estate, I found them gathered here at our house with some other ladies for an Adonis Day celebration. The party was good fun, naturally, and, since I was there anyway, I (*shaking his head sadly*), to my sorrow, stayed and watched. Besides, the racket they were raising kept me from going to sleep. They set up some of the traditional flower pots on the roof, they danced, they made a night of it. scattered all over the place. (*Pauses, then continues reluctantly*)   I hesitate to tell you what happened next. Maybe . . . no, I'm ashamed. It doesn't help any, I know, but I *am* ashamed. (*Falls silent for a moment and then, with a visible effort, blurts out*) Plangon got pregnant! Well, telling you this much just about tells you the act that took place before it. I didn't deny I was the guilty one. In fact, I went on my own to her mother and promised to marry the girl whenever my father got back. I gave my solemn word.

When the baby was born, not long ago, I took it over. By a lucky coincidence, Chrysis also had a baby at the same time—Chrysis is the name [of the woman from Samos] . . .

[About thirty lines are missing at this point. Moschion went on to tell how Chrysis abandoned her child as Demeas had ordered (or perhaps gave birth to a stillborn infant) and how, in order to keep Plangon's shame as secret as possible, he gave Chrysis his own baby to nurse. He was helped in all this by his father's valet Parmeno.

Having completed his recital, Moschion leaves, stage right, to go in search of Parmeno. The next moment Chrysis emerges from Demeas' house. At one point her attention is caught and, looking stage right, she sees Moschion and Parmeno hurrying in her direction.]

CHRYSIS   (*to herself*)   They're coming this way in a hurry. I'll wait and listen to what they're saying. (*Moves to an unobtrusive spot off to the side.*)

(*Moschion and Parmeno enter. Parmeno is breathing hard —he had been running from the waterfront to bring the electrifying news of Demeas' return when he ran into Moschion. Moschion is ashen pale and nervous as a cat.*)

MOSCHION   (*wringing his hands*)   You saw my father with your own eyes, Parmeno?
PARMENO   Are you deaf? Yes!
MOSCHION   And Niceratus?
PARMENO   (*nodding*)   He's here.
MOSCHION   (*gloomily*)   How nice for them.
PARMENO   (*putting an arm around his shoulder encouragingly*)   Come on, be a man and bring up the subject of the marriage right away.
MOSCHION   (*unhappily*)   How? Now that it's so close, I'm scared.
PARMENO   (*backing off and eyeing him narrowly*)   How can you say that?
MOSCHION   (*mumbling*)   I'm ashamed to face my father.
PARMENO   (*shouting in exasperation*)   But what about the girl you did wrong to? What about her mother? (*Scornfully*) Ye gods! Look at him shake! You fairy, you!

(*Chrysis walks downstage from where she has been discretely staying out of sight.*)

CHRYSIS   (*to Parmeno*)   You poor fool, what's the hollering about?

PARMENO   (*swiveling around at the sound of her voice*) So Chrysis is here too. (*To Chrysis*) Are you asking what I'm hollering about? This is ridiculous! I want to get on with the marriage. (*Gesturing towards Moschion*) I want him to quit whining in front of the door here and remember the sworn promise he made. Step up and hold the party, put on the wedding garlands, prepare the wedding cake. Don't you think I have plenty of reason to holler?

MOSCHION   (*unhappily*)   I'll do everything. What more can I say?

CHRYSIS   (*nodding*)   I believe you.

PARMENO   (*to Moschion, with a gesture towards Chrysis*)   Let's let her go on nursing the child just as she's doing and tell him it's hers.

CHRYSIS   (*shrugging*)   Well, why not?

MOSCHION   (*to Chrysis*)   Will my father get mad!

CHRYSIS   (*with an understanding smile*)   He'll get over it. My dear boy, he's madly in love too, just as much as you are. And this gets even the hottest tempers to kiss and make up in no time. And, so far as I'm concerned, I think I'd put up with anything rather than have a nurse in some household [take care of the child]. . . .

[About twenty-five lines are lost here in which Parmeno and Chrysis work out the details. Chrysis will keep on caring for the child, thereby saving Plangon from her straight-laced father's wrath, and will depend on her charm to get Demeas' pardon for disobeying his orders. Moschion will tell Demeas of his promise to marry, and depend on his powers of persuasion to get his father to stomach a union with a girl who has no dowry. Parmenon and Chrysis then enter Demeas' house, leaving Moschion to discuss with the audience the unnerving prospect of breaking the news to his father. Here the text resumes, but only enough of his speech is preserved to let us follow the general sense.]

MOSCHION   Is there anybody alive worse off? Why don't I just hang myself right now? . . . (*Resignedly*) I'll go off some place where I can be alone and rehearse [i.e., what to tell Demeas]. I'd better, with an ordeal like this in front of me!

(*Moschion leaves, stage left. The next moment Demeas and Niceratus enter, stage right.*
They have just come from the waterfront and are still in traveling dress. Demeas' servants follow behind, loaded down with luggage. The two men are alike in age—both are in their late forties or early fifties—but in nothing else. Demeas is expensively dressed, relaxed in manner, and has the look of a man with a well developed sense of humor and a capacity for enjoying life. Niceratus is in threadbare garments, nervous and worried in manner, and has the look of a man who rarely gets enjoyment out of life.)

DEMEAS   (*stopping and addressing the whole group*) Don't you feel already the change a place makes? What a difference between here and that place there with all its annoyances! (*Disgustedly*) The Black Sea! Fat-bellied millionaires, sea food every day, things generally sort of unpleasant, wormwood sauce, all the dishes sharp and spicy —my god! (*Drawing a deep breath*) Here we have the good things pure and simple that poor people enjoy. (*Throwing his arms wide*) Lovely Athens! May you get all you deserve for making us, who love our city, the happiest people in the world! (*To the servants, gesturing towards his door*) Go on inside. (*Shoving along a laggard*) Lost your mind? Stand there and stare at me, will you!

NICERATUS   (*thoughtfully*) One thing in particular about that place got me wondering, Demeas. Sometimes, for long periods on end, you couldn't see the sun. Some heavy air, I suppose, kept things in shadow.

DEMEAS   (*smiling*) No, it's that the sun saw nothing to brag about there. So it gave just enough light for the inhabitants to get by on.

NICERATUS   By god, you're right.

DEMEAS   (*getting businesslike*) Let's leave such things for other people to worry about. Now, about what we were discussing—what do you think we ought to do?

NICERATUS   You mean about the marriage with your
son?
DEMEAS   Exactly.
NICERATUS   I say what I've been saying all along: let's
set the day, do it, and god be with us.
DEMEAS   So it seems a good idea?
NICERATUS   To me at any rate.
DEMEAS   (*slapping him on the back*)   To me too—and
I thought so even before you did.
NICERATUS   (*going into his house*)   Call me when you
come out.

[About fifteen lines are missing, in which Demeas delivered
a soliloquy perhaps explaining to the audience why he was
so willing to marry his son to a penniless girl. It must have
been a compelling reason, for Moschion's whole behaviour is
based on the assumption that his father would never countenance such a match.

Demeas enters his house, leaving the stage empty, and a
chorus comes out to dance an entr'acte.]

ACT II

[Moschion enters, stage left. He has been off practicing
the speech he intends to make to his father. The text resumes
as he recounts what seems to have been a daydream. The
first half a dozen lines or so are fragmentary, and we can
gather only the general sense.]

MOSCHION   (*to the audience*)   I rehearsed what . . .
When I got away from the city, [I dreamed] I held my
wedding party, [invited all my friends] to the banquet,
sent the women to take care of the bath, served out the
cake, . . . hummed "Here comes the bride." (*Disgustedly*)
Silly of me! Now that I've had my fill— (*A noise at the
door of Demeas' house stops him abruptly. He turns to see
Demeas stomping out of the door with a sour expression on
his face*) Oh my god, there's my father! He's heard me!
(*Getting hold of himself, he squares his shoulders, puts on*

a convincing smile of welcome, and approaches Demeas)
Father! Delighted to see you!

DEMEAS   (*embracing him warmly*)   Delighted to see
you, my boy!

MOSCHION   Why so down in the mouth?

DEMEAS   (*all the warmth suddenly vanishing*)   Why? Apparently I didn't realize I had a lawfully married mistress.

MOSCHION   (*blankly*)   Lawfully married? How so? I
don't know what you're talking about.

DEMEAS   Apparently I've had a son, without my knowing
about it. (*Roaring*) But she's getting kicked right out of
the house with it and going straight to hell!

MOSCHION   (*blanching*)   You can't!

DEMEAS   (*savagely*)   What do you mean I can't? You
expect me to raise an illegitimate child? In my own house?
That's not *my* way of doing things!

MOSCHION   (*throwing his arms wide, glibly*)   Dear lord,
what man among us has been born legitimately? What man
has been born a bastard?

DEMEAS   (*scornfully*)   You're joking.

MOSCHION   So help me, I'm dead serious. (*Loftily*) I
think birth doesn't make a particle of difference. If you
look at it the right way, any good man is legitimate, and
any good-for-nothing is also a bastard.

[About thirty lines are lost. Moschion talks his father into
overlooking Chrysis' apparent disobedience and into keeping
the child. Demeas then brings up the subject closest to his
heart: he would like Moschion to marry Niceratus' daughter;
very likely he added the explanation why money was no ob-
ject. Moschion, unable to believe his ears, not only agrees
with alacrity, but presses Demeas to hold the wedding right
away.]

DEMEAS   Are you serious?
MOSCHION   I love her . . .

[The next four lines are too fragmentary to yield sense.]

MOSCHION   I wish you knew how serious I am! I wish

you could help me! (*Gloomily*) But you know nothing about the situation.

DEMEAS   Know nothing about how serious you are? (*Affectionately*) I understand the situation you're talking about perfectly, Moschion. (*Gesturing towards Niceratus' house*) I'm going right over to him and tell him to get on with the wedding. Things at our end will be all set.

MOSCHION   (*hurriedly*)   I'll go inside, wash up, make the libation, put the incense on the altar, and go get the girl. (*Starts off towards Niceratus' house.*)

DEMEAS   (*holding him back*)   Not just yet. Not till I find out if he's agreeable.

MOSCHION   He won't say no to you. (*Starting off again*) I really shouldn't be in on this conference and get in your way. So I'll run along. (*He dashes off, stage left.*)

DEMEAS   (*to the audience, reflectively*)   I guess there exists some patron saint of coincidence who comes to the rescue when you're groping in the dark. Now, I had no idea that Moschion was in love . . .

[There is a gap here of about fifty lines. The first thirty or so are completely gone, the next twenty fragmentary. From these we gather that Niceratus came out and Demeas convinced him to hold the wedding without delay. The text resumes as they plan the shopping for the banquet.]

DEMEAS   (*calling through the door of his house*)   Parmeno! Hey, Parmeno! (*Parmeno comes dashing out.*) Wedding garlands, an animal for the sacrifice, a cake. Take a bag and shop in everything there is in the market.

PARMENO   (*blankly, the news of a wedding taking him by surprise*)   Everything? Me? But, Demeas . . . [A few words are lost here.]

DEMEAS   (*interrupting*)   And quickly. I mean this minute! Bring back a cook too.

PARMENO   A cook too? Hire and bring back a cook?

DEMEAS   Hire and bring back a cook.

PARMENO   I'll take some money and be right off. (*He dashes into Demeas' house.*)

DEMEAS   (*to Niceratus*)   Niceratus, you still here?

NICERATUS   I'll go in and tell my wife to get everything ready inside and then I'll follow right after him (*gesturing toward Parmeno*).

PARMENO   (*reappearing at the door, to the servants inside*)   All I know is what I've been ordered to do, and I'm on my way there right now.

DEMEAS   (*thoughtfully, to himself*)   He'll have trouble convincing his wife. But we can't give them any time for talk. (*Suddenly realizing that Parmeno is still there*) Hey! You hanging around? Run!

[About a dozen lines are lost here. A few belong to the end of Act II, the rest to the beginning of Act III.

At the end of Act II, Demeas entered his house, Parmeno exited stage left, Niceratus followed shortly after, and the chorus came on to perform an entr'acte.]

ACT III

(*Demeas comes out of his house with an elaborate show of being casual, and walks downstage. Suddenly shedding his casual air, he addresses the audience in great perturbation. His opening words have been lost.*)

DEMEAS   . . . the hurricane that suddenly comes out of the blue during a calm voyage—you're sailing along under clear skies, and it smashes right into you and over you go. Sometimes like that is what I'm going through right now. I'm the one who's holding the wedding, who's appeasing all the gods, who just a while ago was having things go exactly the way I wanted—my god, right now I'm not sure any longer whether I can see straight! I'm here before you with a sudden aching hurt in my heart. (*Shaking his head in bewilderment*) It's incredible! Look here. Am I in my right mind? Or am I crazy and, because I jumped to all the wrong conclusions a moment ago, heading for disaster for no good reason?

(*Visibly getting hold of himself, in calmer tones*) As soon as I went inside, since I was very anxious to get on with the wedding, I simply announced to the servants what was going to happen and ordered them to make all the necessary preparations—clean up, do the baking, get everything set for the ceremony. Things were getting done, all right, but naturally, there was some confusion because of the rush. The baby had been sort of left on a couch out of the way and was screaming its head off. And everybody was hollering at the same time: (*imitating the voices*) "Bring some flour. Bring some water. Bring some oil. Bring some charcoal." I pitched in myself and helped hand things out. That's how I happened to go into the pantry and, since I was busy there picking out extra supplies and looking things over, I didn't come right out. Well, while I was in there, one of the women came down from the second floor into the room in front of the pantry. We do our weaving there, and you have to go through it either to get to the staircase or the pantry. It was an old woman who used to be Moschion's nanny; she was one of my slaves until I freed her. She saw the baby screaming away because nobody was minding it and, having no idea that I was inside and that she ought to watch out what she was saying, she goes up to it and starts to talk to it the way they do (*imitating her*): "Sweet little baby," and "My precious, where's your mommy?" And she kissed it and rocked it and, when it stopped crying, she says to herself, "Dear me! It seems just yesterday that I was petting and nursing Moschion when he was no bigger than this, and now he's got a baby of his own." [Two or three lines are lost here.]

While she was prattling on, one of the serving girls came running in, and the old one shouts at her: "Here you! Give this baby a bath! What is this? His own father's getting married, and you're not giving his little one the least bit of attention! Right away the other one whispers to her (*dropping his voice and imitating her*), "What are you talking so loud for, you poor fool? *He's* in there." "No! Where?" "In the pantry!" And then, speaking in her natural voice, she says (*raising his voice*), "Nurse, Chrysis is calling for you" and "Hurry, run along," and then (*lowering it again*), "We're in luck, he hasn't heard anything." So the old one scuttled off somewhere mumbling to herself (*mimicking her*), "Dear me, this big mouth of mine!"

Then I came out, very calmly, just as you saw me come out a moment ago, acting as if I hadn't heard or didn't know a thing. And, right outside, what do I see? Chrysis herself with the baby, nursing it. So one thing we know for certain: it's her baby. But who the father is, I or—no, gentlemen, I'm not going to say it to you, I'm not even going to suspect it. I'm reporting the facts, what I heard with my own ears. I'm not angry with anybody—not yet. (*As the calm he has been struggling to maintain starts to desert him, emphatically*) Good god, I know that boy of mine; he's always been thoroughly decent, always been as considerate toward me as any son could be. (*Shakes his head worriedly.*) Yet, when I consider that it was his old nanny who said it and that it was something I wasn't supposed to hear, and when I look back at the way that woman of mine fondled the child and forced me to let her keep it against my will—I can go out of my mind! (*Looks toward the wings, stage left, and sees someone approaching.*) Good—here comes Parmeno back from the market just in time. But first I've got to let him take in the help he's brought back with him.

(*Demeas steps back to let Parmeno, who is carrying a shopping bag and is followed by a cook and some other servants he has hired in town for the wedding party, pass into the house. They come on stage without noticing Demeas. The cook—whose job included butchering the animals as well as cooking them—is, as always in Greek New Comedy, long-winded and self-important. He has clearly been wagging his jaw all during the walk from the market.*)

PARMENO   (*maliciously*) I swear to god, cook, I don't know why you bother carrying knives around. You can kill anything you want with that tongue of yours.
COOK   (*haughtily*) You miserable idiot!
PARMENO   (*guilelessly*) Who? Me?
COOK   (*as before*) You sure sound like one, believe me.

If I ask a simple question like how many tables you plan to set, how many ladies there'll be, when you want to serve, whether we'll have to take on a waiter, whether you have enough dishes, whether the kitchen is out-of-doors, whether everything else—

PARMENO   Don't you realize it? You're just killing, that's what you are. You slay me. Like an expert.

COOK   Go to the devil!

PARMENO   (*with elaborate politeness*)   You first, by all means. (*To the whole group at his heels*)   Inside everybody!

DEMEAS   (*to Parmeno as he is on the point of following his task force indoors*)   Parmeno!

PARMENO   (*knowing very well it's Demeas calling but anxious to delay the inevitable moment when he will be quizzed on what has been going on, without turning around*)   Somebody calling me?

DEMEAS   Yes, you.

PARMENO   (*turning around reluctantly*)   Oh, hello.

DEMEAS   Take that bag inside and come right back here.

PARMENO   (*to himself fervently as he goes inside*)   Wish me luck!

DEMEAS   (*gesturing toward the departing figure of Parmeno, to the audience*)   If you ask me, whatever's going on around here wouldn't be any secret to that fellow. He knows everybody else's business, if anyone does. There's the door—he's coming out now.

PARMENO   (*turning at the door to talk to Chrysis inside*)   Chrysis, give the cook whatever he asks for. And, for god's sake, keep that old hag of a nurse away from the wine. (*To Demeas, but still standing a safe distance away near the door; with affected cheeriness*)   Now, what would you like?

DEMEAS   What would I like? For you to get away from that door! (*Parmeno takes a minuscule step nearer*) Further!

PARMENO   (*finally giving up and coming near him*)   Here I am.

DEMEAS   (*sternly*)   Now listen, Parmeno. So help me, there are lots of reasons why I don't want to give you a beating—

PARMENO　　(*with a practiced air of innocence*)　A beating? What'd I do?

DEMEAS　　(*emphatically*)　You're hiding something from me. (*As Parmeno opens his mouth to protest*) I've noticed it, all right.

PARMENO　　(*excitedly*)　I swear to god! I swear by all that's holy! I swear on a stack—

DEMEAS　　(*interrupting, curtly*)　Cut it out. Don't do any swearing. I know what I'm talking about.

PARMENO　　(*aggrieved*)　So help me—

DEMEAS　　(*interrupting*)　Look at me!

PARMENO　　(*deflated, knowing the jig is up*)　I am.

DEMEAS　　(*grimly*)　Out with it: Whose baby is it?

PARMENO　　(*in a desperate effort to switch the conversation*)　Hey, look!

DEMEAS　　(*not falling into the trap*)　I'm asking you: Whose baby is it?

PARMENO　　Chrysis'.

DEMEAS　　(*intently*)　And the father?

PARMENO　　She says you are.

DEMEAS　　(*exploding*)　Parmeno, that's the end for you —you're lying to me!

PARMENO　　Who, me?

DEMEAS　　(*with ominous calm*)　Because I found out everything. I know that it's Moschion's; I know that you know it too; and I know that he's the reasons she's taking care of it now.

PARMENO　　(*blustering*)　Who says so?

DEMEAS　　Everybody. Just tell me this—I'm right, yes? (*Steps toward him menacingly.*)

PARMENO　　(*cringing*)　Yes, sir, but to keep it a secret—

DEMEAS　　(*roaring*)　What? Keep it a secret! (*Shouting to the servants in the house*) Inside there! Someone bring me a whip for this godforsaken slave of mine!

PARMENO　　Oh, no! Oh, god, no!

DEMEAS　　(*between his teeth*)　So help me, I'm going to skin you alive.

PARMENO　　Skin me alive?

DEMEAS　　(*as a slave comes out and hands him a whip*) Right now.

PARMENO   (*to himself, agonized*)   I'm a goner! (*Whirls
around and takes off, stage left.*)

DEMEAS   (*shouting after him*)   Hey, you! Where are
you going, you good-for-nothing? (*To the slave*) Go get
him! (*Losing all control, starts wildly quoting passages
from Euripides*)   O Athens built in ancient days, O far-
stretched span of heaven, O— (*Suddenly getting hold of
himself*)   Hey, Demeas, what are you raving for? Gone
mad? What are you raving for, anyway? Get hold of yourself. Buck up. You've got nothing against Moschion. (*To
the audience*)   Gentlemen, this may sound like a risky
thing to say, but it's the truth. Let's suppose Moschion
did what he did with malice aforethought, either because
he hated me or because he was so passionately in love with
her. He'd feel the same way now as he did then, chin out
and spoiling for a fight. But he's cleared himself of all
guilt on that score: when I told him about the marriage
he was honestly glad to hear about it. I thought he was so
eager because he was in love with the girl—but he was
just anxious to escape finally from the clutches of that
Helen of mine in there (*gesturing toward the house*).
She's to blame for what happened. She must have gotten
her hands on him sometime when he was drunk and not
himself. When wine and youth find a willing accomplice right
at hand, a lot of senseless things can come out of the com-
bination. I simply cannot bring myself to believe that a
boy who's so decent and well behaved toward everyone
else would have deliberately acted this way toward me. And
the fact that he's an adopted son doesn't make a particle
of difference; what I look at is not his birth but his character. (*His thoughts shift from Moschion to Chrysis, and
his self-control begins to disintegrate.*)   But that woman's
a whore, a ruination— (*Recovering again*)   What's this
for? It's not going to get you anywhere. Demeas, you've
got to be a man now. Forget this passion of yours, stop
loving her, and, for your son's sake, just do all you can
to hush up this awful thing that's happened. Take that
lovely lady and throw her out on her ear; to hell with her.
You've got a good excuse—because she insisted on keeping

the infant. Don't mention a single thing else. Stiff upper lip and don't weaken. Show what you're made of.

(*As Demeas stands there absorbed in thought, the cook comes out of the door. He's looking for Parmeno.*)

COOK   (*to himself*)   Maybe he's out here in front of the house. Hey! Parmeno! (*Aggrieved*) The man's run out on me. And he didn't even lend a hand for one minute.

DEMEAS   (*suddenly making up his mind, wheels around, charges toward the door and, en route, roars at the cook*) Out of my way!

COOK   (*as he's jostled aside*)   Ye gods! Hey, what is this? (*Rubbing his eyes*) Did an old man run inside like a lunatic just now? Or what the devil is it? (*Shrugging*) What's it to me? (*Thinking over what had just happened*) God almighty, you ask me, it was a lunatic all right. Sure let out one big howl. Now won't it be just fine if he gets into the dishes I've laid out and smashes them all to pieces. (*Demeas' door starts to open.*) Someone's coming out. Parmeno, I'd like to wring your neck for bringing me here! I'll get out of the way over here. (*Moves off to the side where he can stay unobserved.*)

(*The door opens and Demeas and Chrysis clutching the baby in her arms come out.*)

DEMEAS   (*angrily*)   Are you deaf? Get out of here!
CHRYSIS   (*in tears*)   Where in the world can I go?
DEMEAS   Go to the devil!
CHRYSIS   (*sobbing*)   Oh, my god, my god!
DEMEAS   (*mimicking her*)   "Oh, my god, my god." (*Sarcastically*) By all means, let's have tears; always good for some sympathy. (*Mumbling to himself*) I've got an idea I'll keep you from—
CHRYSIS   (*looking up at this first hint of what is causing her banishment*)   Doing what?
DEMEAS   (*remembering, just in time, his decision to stick strictly to the keeping of the infant*)   Nothing. (*Bru-*

tally)   You've got the baby; you've got the nurse. Now
beat it, I say!

CHRYSIS   Just because I insisted on keeping the child?

DEMEAS   For that and—

CHRYSIS   (*interrupting*) And what?

DEMEAS   For that, period.

COOK   (*aside, gesturing toward the two figures*)   So this
is the sort of trouble it is. I get it.

DEMEAS   (*abandoning his resolution and casting about,
guiltily, for some stronger justification*)   Well, you didn't
know how to fit in with people of my class.

CHRYSIS   (*startled*)   I didn't know what? What's that
you say?

DEMEAS   Look here, Chrysis, you haven't forgotten that
when you came here you had only the clothes on your back.

CHRYSIS   What about it?

DEMEAS   Back in those days, when you were down on
your luck, I was everything to you.

CHRYSIS   (*humbly*)   Have I changed?

DEMEAS   (*aware that he is getting into just what he
wanted to avoid, and shamed by her attitude*)   Enough of
this talk. You've got everything that's yours. I'm even
adding servants. Now leave the house.

COOK   (*nodding sagely to himself*)   One of these cases
of a man losing his temper. (*Self-importantly*) I'd better go
up to him. (*Coming forward and addressing Demeas*) I
beg your pardon, but you ought to watch out that—

DEMEAS   (*turning on him*)   What are you butting in
for?

COOK   (*taken aback*)   You don't have to bite my head
off!

DEMEAS   (*disregarding him and turning back to Chrysis*)   Some other girl will be very glad to take your place,
Chrysis, and thank her lucky stars too.

COOK   (*aside, puzzled*)   Who's that?

DEMEAS   (*Bitterly*)   But you've got yourself a son.
Now you've got everything.

COOK   (*to himself*)   Hasn't bitten me yet. (*Going up
to Demeas again*) I beg your—

DEMEAS (*roaring*) If you butt in again, I'll break your skull!

COOK (*muttering*) If I butt in again, I deserve it. See? I'm going right inside. (*Scuttles through the door of Demeas' house.*)

DEMEAS (*to Chrysis*) Big shot, aren't you? Wait till you start living on the town—you'll see yourself as you really are. Other girls in your situation, Chrysis, to make a few dollars to keep alive become call girls and drink themselves to death. And if they're not willing and quick about it, they starve to death. Nobody will learn this lesson better than you, I know it. And you'll learn what kind of woman you are and what a mistake you made. (*As she goes near to him to plead*) Stay where you are! (*He stalks into the house and slams the door.*)

(*Niceratus enters stage left, leading a sheep on a rope. The animal, which he is supplying for the formal sacrifice at the wedding and which, after being offered up, will supply the meat course at the banquet, is a distinctly scrawny specimen; as Niceratus' descriptions reveals, it has everything except flesh.*)

NICERATUS (*to himself, not noticing the forlorn figure of Chrysis*) This sheep will very nicely take care of all that's required for the gods once it's sacrificed. The goddesses too. It's got blood, plenty of bile, good bones, big spleen—it'll satisfy the celestial requirements. I'll make hash out of the skin to send as a present to my friends; (*dolefully*) that's all there'll be left of it for me. (*Catching sight of Chrysis*) My god, what is this? That can't be Chrysis crying there in front of the door. It is, at that. (*Going up to her*) What in the world is the matter?

CHRYSIS (*bitterly*) That fine friend of yours has thrown me out. What else?

NICERATUS My god! Who? Demeas?

CHRYSIS Yes.

NICERATUS On account of what?

CHRYSIS On account of the child.

NICERATUS   (*unsympathetically*)   Yes, I heard from
my womenfolk that you had insisted on keeping an infant
and were raising it. Crazy idea! He's a push-over, that man.
CHRYSIS   He didn't get angry at first. It was only after
a while, just now. First he tells me to get things ready inside for the wedding and then, right in the middle of
everything, he rushes in at me like a lunatic and shuts the
door on me!
NICERATUS   He's touched in the head. (*Shaking his
head*)   Not a healthy place, that Black Sea area. Come
inside here with me to my wife. (*As Chrysis breaks into
fresh sobs*) Cheer up! What more do you want? The time
will come when he'll realize what he's doing, and then he'll
get over this lunacy and stop.

(*Niceratus leads Chrysis into his house. The stage is now
empty, and the chorus comes out and performs an entr'acte.*)

ACT IV

(*Niceratus comes out of his house.*)

NICERATUS   (*through the door to his wife inside*)
You'll be the death of me! I'll go now and tackle him.
(*Muttering to himself*) God in heaven, even for a king's
ransom, I wouldn't have had this happen! What an omen
to get just when we're holding a wedding: someone kicked
out of her own house turning up on your doorstep with a
child, everybody in tears, the women all upset. Demeas
is being a stinker. I swear to god, he's going to be sorry for
being such a fool!

(*Moschion enters, stage left. Still hardly believing his
lucky stars, he is nervous as a cat, he cannot wait to get the
wedding over and done with.*)

MOSCHION   (*to the audience*)   The sun is just never
going to go down. What else can you say? The night's
forgot all about itself! Lord, this afternoon is endless! I'll

go and take my third bath. What else have I got to do? (*Starts to go off, stage left.*)

NICERATUS   (*calling*) Moschion! Hello there!

MOSCHION   (*too absorbed in his own affairs to return the cordial greeting*) We're holding the wedding now, right? Parmeno ran into me at the market just now and told me so. Any reason I shouldn't go get your daughter right away?

NCERATUS   (*throwing up his hands*) You've come here without knowing what's going on in there (*gesturing towards Demeas' house*)?

MOSCHION   What's going on?

NICERATUS   What's going on? Something sort of unpleasant has just happened. Something very strange.

MOSCHION   (*nervously*) For god's sakes, what? I've just come, I don't know a thing.

NICERATUS   My dear boy, a minute ago your father kicked Chrysis out of the house.

MOSCHION   (*blanching*) What's that you say?

NICERATUS   (*dolefully*) What happened.

MOSCHION   On account of what?

NICERATUS   On account of the child.

MOSCHION   And where is she now?

NICERATUS   In our house.

MOSCHION   This is incredible! It's terrible!

NICERATUS   If *you* think it's terrible—

(*He is interrupted by a hullaballoo at Demeas' door. The door flies open and Demeas bursts out.*)

DEMEAS   (*shouting to the servants inside, who have obviously dropped everything to bewail Chrysis' abrupt and unhappy departure*) Just let me get my hands on a club, and I'll get those tears out of you! What is this nonsense? Are you going to do what the cook says or not? You have plenty to cry about, all right. You had a very good thing going, while she was in the house. (*Grimly*) The facts speak for themselves! (*He walks downstage a few paces and stops before a statue of Apollo in front of the house*) Dear God, I pray you, please bless this wedding we are now going

to hold. (*Turning to the audience*) Because, gentlemen,
I'm swallowing my anger. I'm going to hold the wedding.
(*Turning back to the statue*) Lord, watch over me so I
don't give myself away to anybody! And give me the
strength to join in on the wedding hymn! [A half line
is lost here.]

NICERATUS   (*sotto voce, to Moschion*) Moschion, you
go up to him first.

MOSCHION   (*walking up to Demeas, frantically*)
Father, what are you doing this for?

DEMEAS   (*coolly*) Doing what?

MOSCHION   You have to ask? Tell me why Chrysis has
left us.

DEMEAS   (*to the audience*) My god—sending an envoy
to see me! This is bad. (*To Moschion*) Damn it all, it's
none of your business. It concerns me, me alone. (*To the
audience*) What is this nonsense? This *is* bad: now he's
joined her, he's doing me wrong too.

MOSCHION   What's that you say?

DEMEAS   (*to the audience*) Clear as day. Else why
does he come here to take her part against me? Of course—
the very thing he has to do.

MOSCHION   Listen, Father. What do you expect your
friends will say when they hear about this?

DEMEAS   Listen, Moschion. You leave my friends to me.

MOSCHION   (*putting on an air of great concern*) I
couldn't look myself in the face if I let you do it.

DEMEAS   (*truculently*) Well, are you going to stop me?

MOSCHION   Yes!

DEMEAS   See here, this is the limit! Bad as it's been up
to now, this is even worse!

MOSCHION   (*loftily*) It's not right to indulge our anger
in everything.

NICERATUS   (*who has been steadily edging nearer the
two to hear what's going on*) Demeas, he's right.

MOSCHION (*to Niceratus*) Niceratus, go inside and tell
her to hurry right back to our house!

DEMEAS   (*shouting*) Moschion, you let me alone! Let
me alone, I tell you! For the third time I'll say it: I know
everything!

MOSCHION   (*nervously, but keeping up a brave front*)
Everything about what?

DEMEAS   (*curtly*)   Don't you talk to me!

MOSCHION   (*in desperation*)   But I have to, Father!

DEMEAS   Have to? Am I to be in charge of my own affairs or not?

MOSCHION   Do me this one favor.

DEMEAS   What favor? (*Icily*)   Maybe you think *I*
should be the one to get out of the house and let you stay,
seeing there are two of you? Let me hold the wedding.
Just let me hold the wedding, if you've got any sense.

MOSCHION   But I *am* letting you! It's just that I want
Chrysis to be there.

DEMEAS   Chrysis, eh?

MOSCHION   (*glibly*)   I want it very much—for your
sake.

DEMEAS   (*to the world at large*)   Isn't it clear? Isn't it
clear as day? God in heaven, I call you to witness this:
someone's in league with my enemies. I'm so mad I'm
going to burst!

MOSCHION   What are you talking about?

DEMEAS   You want me to tell you?

MOSCHION   Yes I do.

DEMEAS   Oh, come on!

MOSCHION   Tell me!

DEMEAS   (*eyeing him narrowly*)   All right, I will. The
child is yours. I know it. I got it from Parmeno, who's
in on your secrets. So don't try any funny stuff on me.

MOSCHION   (*bewildered*)   Then what have you got
against Chrysis, if the child's mine?

DEMEAS   Who should I blame then? You?

MOSCHION   What did she do that's wrong?

DEMEAS   (*roaring*)   What's that you say? Don't you
two have any brains?

MOSCHION   What are you shouting for?

DEMEAS   What am I shouting for, you scum? You have
to ask? Are you taking the blame on yourself? Speak up!
Do you have the gall to look me in the eye and tell me this?
Is this how you happen to have rejected me, this utterly
and completely?

MOSCHION   (*blankly*)   I? What for?

DEMEAS   What for? Do you have to ask that question!

MOSCHION   (*still puzzled*)   After all, what I did isn't absolutely the worst thing in the world. Thousands of fellows have done it, you know.

DEMEAS   (*exploding*)   God in heaven! What gall! (*Between his teeth*) I'm putting the question to you in front of all who are present: who's the mother of that child of yours? Go on, tell it to Niceratus, if you think it's not such a terrible thing.

MOSCHION   (*frantically*)   But it is a terrible thing for me to tell *him*! Is he going to be mad when he hears it!

(*Niceratus looks from Demeas to Moschion in utter bewilderment. Suddenly a light dawns—the same one that had dawned in Demeas' imagination.*)

NICERATUS   (*roaring*)   You are the lowest of the low! Now I'm beginning to get an inkling of what's hit us, of the ungodly thing that's happened!

MOSCHION   (*moaning*)   This means I'm done for.

DEMEAS   Now you understand, eh, Niceratus?

NICERATUS   (*as before*)   Who wouldn't! The worst thing in the world a man could do! (*To Moschion*) Oedipus' incest, Tereus', Thyestes', the incest of all the others we're ever heard about, you've made them all look piddling, you—

MOSCHION   (*interrupting*)   Me?

NICERATUS   You had the brass, the unmitigated gall, to do a thing like that! (*Turning to Demeas*) Demeas, you've got to get just as mad as Amyntor [1] did and put this boy's eyes out!

DEMEAS   (*to Moschion, bitterly*)   Thanks to you, he knows the whole story now!

NICERATUS   (*to Moschion*)   Is there any woman you'd keep your hands off? [A half line is lost here.] And I'm to let you marry my own daughter? I'd sooner—knock wood

---

[1] Amyntor, a mythological character, was in exactly the same position as Demeas imagines he is: his son Phoenix had had relations with his mistress. He punished Phoenix by blinding him.

and fingers crossed—have a son-in-law like Diomnestus,[2] disaster in the flesh!

DEMEAS   (*to Niceratus*)   Though he did me wrong, I kept it to myself.

NICERATUS   (*to Demeas*)   What are you anyway, some miserable slave? If he had disgraced *my* bed, he wouldn't have disgraced another in his life, he or his bedmate. The very next morning, I'd be the first man in history to sell a wife off as a whore and disown a son at the same time. There wouldn't be an empty barber shop or arcade in the city; everybody in town would be sitting there, from the crack of dawn on, talking about me, saying that Niceratus is a real man, someone who takes justice in his hands and prosecutes murder.

MOSCHION   *Murder!*

NICERATUS   (*in ringing tones*)   Acts of this kind, which are done by people who are in revolt against society, *I* call murder!

MOSCHION   (*aside*)   God in heaven, he's got me scared stiff! I'm sunk!

NICERATUS   (*throwing up his hands*)   And, on top of everything else, I took the woman who did such things in under my own roof!

DEMEAS   Niceratus, kick her out! Please! Be big enough to share my wrongs, the way a friend should.

NICERATUS   (*to Demeas, nodding*)   Yes, even though just looking at her will make me burst! (*As he starts toward his door, Moschion comes before him pleadingly*) Are you looking at me, you barbarian? You're a wild Indian, that's what you are! (*Icily*) Kindly let me pass!

(*Niceratus stalks off into his house. Moschion stands dumbly for a moment. Suddenly he smites his brow and, galvanized, turns to Demeas.*)

MOSCHION   Father, in god's name, listen to me—

DEMEAS   (*interrupting*)   I'm not listening to a word from you.

[2] Perhaps an allusion to some contemporary notorious ne'er-do-well.

MOSCHION   It's nothing like what you imagine! I just
realized what's going on.
DEMEAS   (*coldly*) "Nothing like", eh? How's that?
MOSCHION   (*blurting it out*) Chrysis isn't the mother
of that baby she's taking care of right now. She's saying
it's hers as a favor to me.
DEMEAS   What's that you say?
MOSCHION   The truth.
DEMEAS   But why this favor?
MOSCHION   (*sighing*) I hate to tell you. But if you get
the whole story of what happened, I avoid the blame for
something serious and take it for just something minor.
DEMEAS   (*exasperated*) You'll kill me before you get
a word out!
MOSCHION   I got Niceratus' daughter pregnant. But I
wanted to keep it a secret.

(*There is a moment's silence as Demeas stares at him taking in the implications of what the boy has said.*)

DEMEAS   What's that you say?
MOSCHION   What happened.
DEMEAS   I warn you—don't try any tricks on me!
MOSCHION   About something you can prove for yourself?
What would I gain?
DEMEAS   (*impressed*) Nothing. (*Hearing a noise at
Niceratus' door*) Hey, someone's coming out.

(*The door flies open and Niceratus bursts out, a stricken
man. He staggers downstage and addresses the audience.*)

NICERATUS   Oh my god, my god! What a sight I saw!
I couldn't wait to get out the door—I'm going mad, I've
been struck to the heart by a bolt from the blue!
DEMEAS   (*sotto voce to Moschion*) What in the world is
he talking about?
NICERATUS   Just now I caught my daughter nursing the
baby in there.
MOSCHION   (*sotto voce to Demeas, triumphantly*)
There you are! You hear that, Father?

DEMEAS (*sotto voce to Moschion, jubilantly*) You're not the guilty one Moschion. I'm the guilty one for suspecting you of such things!

NICERATUS (*interrupting, as he turns from the audience and heads toward Demeas*) Demeas, I'm coming to see you.

MOSCHION (*sotto voce to Demeas*) I'm getting out of here!

DEMEAS (*sotto voce to Moschion*) Cheer up!

MOSCHION (*as he races off, stage left*) One look at him and I'm a dead man!

DEMEAS (*to Niceratus, brightly*) What's the trouble?

NICERATUS I just now caught my daughter nursing the baby inside.

DEMEAS (*as before*) Maybe it was a joke.

NICERATUS (*shaking his head vigorously*) It was no joke, because the minute she saw me come in she went into a panic.

DEMEAS (*reassuringly*) Maybe it just looked that way to you.

NICERATUS (*grumbling*) You'll kill me with this saying "maybe" to everything.

DEMEAS (*to himself, ruefully*) This is all my fault!

NICERATUS What are you saying?

DEMEAS In my opinion, you're telling me something that's simply unbelievable.

NICERATUS But I saw it!

DEMEAS Nonsense!

NICERATUS (*exasperated*) This is no fairy story! I'm going back inside— (*Without finishing his sentence, he whirls about and heads for his door.*)

DEMEAS (*calling*) I say there, wait a second, please! (*As Niceratus disappears into the house*) He's gone. (*Throwing up his hands*) This is the end. Everything's topsy-turvy. My god, will he be mad when he hears what really happened! He'll howl! He's tough and he's rough, the kind that wants everything his own way. (*Shaking his head in remorse*) How could I have had such suspicions? I must have a filthy mind. God, I deserve to be killed! (*There's a roar from inside Niceratus' house.*) God al-

mighty, listen to him howl! (*Goes to the door and puts his
ear to it. Listens, then incredulously*) There you are—he's
yelling for fire. (*Listening again*) He's threatening to burn
the baby up alive. I'll be looking at my grandson cooking!
There's the door again. (*Scuttles away as the door is flung
open and Niceratus bursts out.*) The man's a hurricane,
I swear.

NICERATUS   (*excitedly*) Demeas! Chrysis is starting a
revolution against me. She's making terrible trouble.

DEMEAS   What's that you say?

NICERATUS   She's talked my wife into denying everything. My daughter too. She's keeping the baby from me;
says she won't give it up. (*Between his teeth*) So don't
be surprised if I murder her with my own hands.

DEMEAS   (*genuinely alarmed*) Murder her?

NICERATUS   Sure. She knows the whole story.

DEMEAS   Niceratus! Don't do it!

NICERATUS   (*over his shoulder as he rushes back into
the house*) I just wanted to warn you.

DEMEAS   (*to himself*) He's out of his mind—there he
goes galloping off again. (*Worriedly*) What do you do in
a case like this? So help me, I know I've never gotten into
a mess like this before. (*Shaking his head ruefully*) The
best idea is to make a clean breast of what's happened, no
question about it. My god, there goes the door again!

(*Niceratus' door flies open, and Chrysis bursts out, clutching the baby. In her rush she doesn't notice Demeas.*)

CHRYSIS   (*screaming*) In the name of heaven, what am
I to do? Where can I run? He'll take my child from me!

DEMEAS   (*shouting*) Chrysis! This way!

CHRYSIS   Who's there?

DEMEAS   Inside with you!

(*She ducks behind him, and Demeas plants himself in front
of her just in time to intercept Niceratus who comes running
out of his house brandishing a club.*)

NICERATUS   (*shouting, to Chrysis*)   Hey you? Where
are you running to?

DEMEAS   (*aside*)   So help me, it looks as if I'm going
to be a sparring partner today. (*To Niceratus*) What's the
hurry? Who are you after?

NICERATUS   (*between his teeth*)   Demeas, out of my
way. I'm going to get that baby and get the story out of
those women, and don't try to stop me.

DEMEAS   No, you're not. (*He squares off to slug it out if
need be.*)

NICERATUS   (*snarling*)   So you want to fight, eh?

DEMEAS   I sure do. (*To Chrysis, who is lingering hesi-
tantly behind him*)   Get the hell inside, quick!

NICERATUS   That's just what I want too.

DEMEAS   (*as he starts flailing away*)   Chrysis! Run!
He's stronger than I am!

(*Chrysis scoots into Demeas' house and, a second later, the
two oldsters, out of breath, stand apart glowering at each
other. Demeas has succeeded in keeping his back to his door.*)

NICERATUS   (*accusingly*)   You're the one who's starting the hitting. I'm a witness.

DEMEAS   And you're taking a stick to a respectable
woman and chasing after her.

NICERATUS   You're a liar!

DEMEAS   You're another!

(*Another moment of silence as they puff and glare.*)

NICERATUS   Give me the baby.

DEMEAS   Don't be ridiculous! It's mine.

NICERATUS   It is not!

DEMEAS   It is so.

NICERATUS   (*at the top of his lungs*)   Help!

DEMEAS   Holler your head off.

NICERATUS   (*screaming in impotent rage*)   I'm going
inside and kill that woman! It's all I can do!

DEMEAS   (*to the world at large*)   Here we go again.

(*To Niceratus*) I'm not going to put up with this. (*As Niceratus again tries to shove his way to the door*) Where do you think you're going? Stand back!

NICERATUS Don't you dare raise your hand to me!

DEMEAS Then get hold of yourself.

NICERATUS Demeas, you're out to do me wrong, I can see it. What's more, you know the whole story.

DEMEAS (*testily*)) Then ask me about it and stop being a nuisance to that woman.

NICERATUS Has that son of yours pulled a fast one on me?

DEMEAS (*hurriedly*) Stop talking nonsense. He's going to marry the girl. It's nothing like that. (*Soothingly*) Let's you and I take a little walk over here.

NICERATUS (*taken aback*) Take a walk?

DEMEAS And you can pull yourself together.

(*Demeas takes the bemused Niceratus by the arm and starts walking him up and down the stage. Demeas, completely his old self, has a mischievous glint in his eye as he chats with his slower-witted neighbor.*)

DEMEAS Tell me, Niceratus, you've seen that play, haven't you, the one that tells how Zeus once turned himself into a golden shower, trickled down through the roof of a house, and seduced a girl shut up inside? [1]

NICERATUS (*puzzled*) Well, what about it?

DEMEAS Maybe we have to be ready to expect anything. Think now: Do you have any leaks in your roof?

NICERATUS Lots. But what's that got to do with it?

DEMEAS Sometimes Zeus turns himself into gold. Other times into water. See? He's responsible for what happened. Lucky thing we discovered it so quickly.

NICERATUS (*still puzzled by Demeas' straight face, but growing suspicious*) Are you kidding me?

DEMEAS So help me, I'm not. I'd say you're in exactly the same situation Acrisius was. If his daughter had the honor of a visit from Zeus, your daughter—

[1] He is referring to the mythological story of Danae, the daughter of Acrisius.

NICERATUS   (*interrupting*)   God almighty! Moschion's pulled a fast one on me!

DEMEAS   (*quickly*)   He'll marry her! Stop worrying! (*resuming his former soothing tone*) Take my word for it, this was a celestial visitation. You think it's something amazing, but I can name thousands of these celestially sired children walking around in our very midst. First of all, take Chaerophon. He scrounges a life of luxury without paying a cent. You have to have divine blood in you to do that, right?

NICERATUS   (*resignedly*)   Right. (*Shrugging*) What can I do? I'm not going to argue with you over nothing at all.

DEMEAS   (*nodding approvingly*)   Very sensible remark, Niceratus. Take Androcles. Look how old he is. Yet he still goes out on the town, runs around, does plenty of scrounging, and keeps his white hair nice and black. You couldn't kill him off even if you slit his throat. Another case of divine blood, right? (*Guiding him toward his door*) Now run along and pray that everything will be all right. Start the ceremony. My son's coming to get your daughter right away. (*With a knowing shake of the head*) It's all Fate's doing.

NICERATUS   (*abstractedly*)   So many things are.

DEMEAS   Very sensible remark.

NICERATUS   (*flaring up again*)   If he was caught then—

DEMEAS   (*interrupting hurriedly*)   None of that! No getting yourself all hot and bothered. Go inside and make sure everything is all set.

NICERATUS   I will.

DEMEAS   And I'll take care of things at my end.

NICERATUS   Do that. (*Goes inside his house.*)

DEMEAS   (*calling after him*)   You're a smart fellow. (*To himself*) Thank the good lord none of my suspicions turned out to be true!

(*Demeas enters his house. The stage is now clear, and the chorus enters and dances an entr'acte.*)

ACT V

(Moschion enters, stage left. He has something on his mind —and makes his way downstage to unburden himself to the audience.)

MOSCHION   When I was cleared of that false accusation a little while ago, I felt pretty good about it. I figured I got a lucky break, and I was satisfied with it. But now that I've had time to collect my wits and know what the score is, I'm really burned up. It drives me crazy—my father was willing to believe I could stoop so low! If the girl's situation was all right, and if there weren't a lot of things that keep me tied down—I gave her my word, we've known each other so long and so intimately, and I love her—he wouldn't have a second chance to make such accusations, at least to my face. I'd clear out of Athens; I'd be off in Asia with the foreign legion there. But no, I'm not going to go off and make a name for myself, and all for your sake, Plangon, my sweetheart. I can't—because I'm a slave now of the love for you in my heart. *(Falls silent for a moment, building up his righteous indignation)* But I simply can't sit back like some spineless clod and take no notice of it. *(Brightening as he gets an idea)* Even if it's just a bluff and nothing else, I want to give my father a scare. I'm going to tell him I'm going away. When he sees I'm dead serious about what he did this time, he'll think twice before he's unfair with me hereafter. *(Notices Parmeno entering, stage left.)* Well, look who's here, just in time. Just the man I want.

PARMENO   *(not noticing Moschion, to himself)*   God almighty, that was a miserably stupid stunt I pulled. Absolutely innocent, and yet I got scared and ran away from Demeas. And what'd I do to be scared about? Let's examine the record, item by item. Moschion seduces a respectable girl—*(grinning)* nothing you can charge Parmeno with there, of course. She gets pregnant—Parmeno not guilty.

The baby goes into our house—*he* brought it in, not I. Someone in the household agreed to play mother to it. What did Parmeno do wrong there? Nothing. So why did you get so panicky and run away like that, stupid? Don't be ridiculous! He said he'd skin you alive. Understand? Doesn't make a particle of difference whether you deserved it or not, skinning's no fun, no fun at all.

MOSCHION   Hey!

PARMENO   (*turning*)   Oh, hello.

MOSCHION   Cut out the jabbering and go inside. Quick!

PARMENO   To do what?

MOSCHION   Bring me an overcoat and a sword.

PARMENO   (*not believing his ears*)   A sword? For you?

MOSCHION   And make it snappy.

PARMENO   What for?

MOSCHION   Shut up. Go and do as you're told.

PARMENO   But what's up?

MOSCHION   (*taking a threatening step toward him*)   If I get my hands on a whip——

PARMENO   (*with alacrity*)   No, sir! I'm going! (*Doesn't move.*)

MOSCHION   (*shouting*)   What are you waiting for? (*Parmeno hustles into the house. Moschion continues, to himself.*) My father's sure to come out now and plead with me to stay. I'll let him plead away for a while; that much I've got to do. Then, when it looks like the right moment, I'll give in. The important thing is to sound as if I meant it. (*His courage ebbing*) Oh, my god, that's the one thing I can't do! (*Listening at the door*) I thought so—he's coming out now.

(*The door opens but it is Parmeno, not Demeas, who comes out, and he is empty-handed.*)

PARMENO   (*earnestly*)   I think you're way behind the times; you don't know what's going on inside. You haven't heard the right story, and you're giving up and getting yourself in an uproar for no good reason.

MOSCHION   (*grimly*)   Where are my things?

PARMENO   (*disregarding the question and continuing as before*)   Your wedding's going on (*Carried away by the spirit of the occasion*) They're killing the fatted calf—
MOSCHION   (*ominously*)   Listen, you—where are my things?
PARMENO   (*again disregarding the question*)   They're waiting for you, just for you. Been waiting a long time. Aren't you going to come for your bride? You're a lucky fellow! Everything's going fine. Buck up! What more do you want?
MOSCHION   (*advancing on him*)   Are you telling me what to do, you good-for-nothing?
PARMENO   (*alarmed*)   Hey, Moschion! What are you doing!
MOSCHION   (*slapping him hard*)   Now are you going to hurry in there and bring me the things I told you to?
PARMENO   You cut my lip!
MOSCHION   Are you still blabbering?
PARMENO   (*quickly*)   I'm going. (*To the world at large*) God almighty, I had to run into this trouble!
MOSCHION   (*menacingly*)   Still hanging around?
PARMENO   (*making a last desperate attempt*)   I tell you, they're really holding the wedding.
MOSCHION   Again? (*Chasing him inside*) You bring me back a different report! (*To the audience*) My father'll come out now. (*Struck by a new thought*) But, gentlemen, what if he doesn't plead with me to stay? What if he gets angry and lets me go? I didn't think of that before. What am I going to do? (*Reassuring himself*) But he wouldn't do a thing like that. But supposing he does? After all, anything can happen. God almighty, if I do an about-face now, I'll look like a fool!

(*The door of Demeas' house opens stealthily, and Parmeno appears, holding an overcoat and sword, with Demeas behind him; he has alerted Demeas to what is going on. He points to Moschion; Demeas nods his understanding and disappears back into the house.*)

PARMENO   (*coming forward*)   Here you are. Overcoat and sword. Take them.

MOSCHION   Hand them over. (*As he takes them*)   No one inside saw you?

PARMENO   (*guilelessly*)   Noone.

MOSCHION   Noone at all?

PARMENO   (*blandly*)   That's right.

MOSCHION   What's that you say? (*In baffled rage*)   God damn you to hell!

PARMENO   (*shrugging*)   Lead on wherever you're going. You're not making sense.

(*The door to Demeas' house opens and Demeas appears in the doorway.*)

DEMEAS   (*through the doorway as if to someone inside*)   Then tell me where he is. (*Turning and catching sight of Parmeno and Moschion, with a great air of being surprised*) Hey, what is this?

PARMENO   (*to Moschion*)   Hurry up, lead on!

DEMEAS   (*to Moschion*)   Why the coat? What's the matter? Moschion, tell me, are you about to go away?

PARMENO   (*with an air of finality*)   As you see, he's off, he's on his way. (*To Moschion, all innocence*)   Got to say a word to the people inside. I'll go right now. (*He dashes off into Niceratus' house.*)

DEMEAS   Moschion, you're angry—and I love you for it, I don't at all hold it against you. If you've been hurt because of an unjust accusation, it's all my fault. Yet, there's this to keep in mind. . . I'm your father. I adopted you as my son and brought you up. If . . . life has been easy for you, I'm the one who's responsible. And, for my sake, you must swallow what you suffered at my hands and bear with me, the way a son should. I accused you of something falsely. I was ignorant of the facts, I was not in my right mind, I made a mistake. But never forget this: when I made my mistake, I had due regard for you in the eyes of others and I kept to myself whatever it was that, in my ignorance, I committed, I didn't reveal it to any enemies

to give them a chance to crow. But now you're airing my
mistake in public, you're getting people who can bear witness against me about the stupid way I acted. I don't think
that's fair, Moschion. Don't concentrate your memory on
the one day in my life I made a slip and forget all the days
before that. (*Shrugging despondently as he notes Moschion's stony face*) I have lots to tell you, but I'll skip it.
For it's no good for a father to get grudging obedience; it
should be given willingly. Don't forget that.

(*Niceratus appears in the doorway of his house.*)

NICERATUS   (*through the doorway to his wife inside*)
Don't bother me. Everything's taken care of: bath, sacri-
fice, ceremony. So off he goes with his bride whenever he
gets here. (*Turning and catching sight of Demeas and
Moschion*) Hey, what is this?
DEMEAS   (*shrugging despondently*)   So help me, I don't
know.
NICERATUS   What do you mean, you don't know? An
overcoat! This fellow's planning to go off on a trip
somewhere!
DEMEAS   So he says.
NICERATUS   Oh he does, does he. And who's going to
let him—a seducer, a caught and confessed seducer! (*To
Moschion*) I'm going to have you tied up. Right now, this
very minute!
MOSCHION   (*icily*)   By all means. Please do.
NICERATUS   (*exasperated*)   Still talking drivel to me!
You put that sword down this minute!
DEMEAS   (*irritated*)   For god's sake, Moschion, put it
down. Don't provoke him.
MOSCHION   (*quickly putting it down*)   Since you two
have begged me so hard, down it goes.
NICERATUS   Begged you? Oh, come on!
MOSCHION   (*to Niceratus*)   Perhaps you'd like to tie
me up?
DEMEAS   (*to Moschion*)   No, no, no! (*To Niceratus*)
Bring the bride out here.

NICERATUS   (*doubtfully*)   Is it all right?
DEMEAS   Absolutely.

(*Niceratus dashes into his house.*)

MOSCHION   (*sulkily*)   Why didn't you do this right off?
You'd have been spared the trouble of lecturing me just
now.

(*The door of Niceratus' house opens, and he comes out
leading the bride and followed by his wife and a group of
servants.*)

NICERATUS   (*to his daughter*)   You come along with
me. (*As they come up to Moschion*) I hereby give you this
woman to be your lawfully wedded wife and, as her dowry,
my entire estate when I—god forbid!—should die.
MOSCHION   I accept this woman to love, honor and
cherish.
DEMEAS   (*heaving a sigh of relief*)   All that's left to
do is arrange the bath. (*Going to the door of his house
and calling through it*) Chrysis, send along the maids, a
girl for the bath, and a flute player. And someone bring
us a torch and garlands so we can hold the wedding
march.
MOSCHION   (*as a servant comes running out*)   Here
they are.
DEMEAS   (*to Moschion*)   Put one on. (*Eyeing his non-
descript get-up*) And tidy yourself up.
MOSCHION   (*putting on a garland*)   All right.
DEMEAS   (*putting on a garland and stepping forward to
address the audience*)   All of you—young, middle-aged,
old—let's have what brings joy to an actor's heart, the
sign of your good will, a hearty round of applause. And may
the immortal Goddess of Victory, co-sponsor of these splen-
did performances, be on our side forever!

The Shield

DRAMATIS PERSONAE

CLEOSTRATUS, a young man of Athens who has gone off
to the wars to seek his fortune

DAVUS, valet and orderly of Cleostratus (slave)

SMICRINES, an avaricious elderly citizen of Athens, uncle
of Cleostratus

CHAERESTRATUS, a generous elderly citizen of Athens,
younger brother of Smicrines, uncle of Cleostratus

CHAEREAS, stepson of Chaerestratus, in love with Cleostratus' sister

A COOK

A WAITER

A FAKE DOCTOR

SCENE

A street in Athens. Two houses, Smicrines' and Chaerestratus', front on it. The exit on stage left leads downtown,
that on stage right to the waterfront.

ACT I

(*Davus enters, stage right, leading a file of forlorn men,
women, and children. These are captives of war who fell to
the lot of his master Cleostratus; some are carrying bundles.*

Davus is is his middle forties; his face is that of a man you can utterly trust—but not the face of a fool; there are very few who can put anything over on Davus. He is dressed in dusty and worn travel clothes and clutches tightly a battered shield. Wearily and dispiritedly, he leads his group to the middle of the stage, where he turns and addresses the audience. The first fifteen lines of his speech are lost; in these he very likely introduced himself, identified the group he was leading, and explained the reason for his unprepossessing appearance.)

DAVUS *(apostrophizing the master who, so far as he knows, is dead)* Cleostratus, at this moment I am living through [the saddest day of my life]. And my thoughts are far from the hopes I had the day I left. For I pictured you happily safe and sound after the campaign was over, and spending the rest of your days in a life of ease with an appointment as commanding officer or trusted counselor to someone. I pictured you returning home to those who missed you so and giving your sister in marriage—after all, it was for her sake that you went off—to a man like yourself. I pictured myself, as I entered old age, finding my devotion rewarded by rest after my never-ending hardships. But now you've gone off, you've been suddenly snatched away from us, and I, your servant since you were a boy, am the one who has come back—with your shield, which time and again you kept safe but which did not keep you safe. *(Sighing)* Ah, you were a man with a great heart, if ever there was one.

(While Davus is speaking, the door of Smicrines' house opens and Smicrines comes out. He is in his sixties, but looks even older. His clothes are cheap and ill-fitting, his figure is bent and gaunt, his face is a mirror of craftiness and avarice. As he listens intently, his eyes glisten. The minute Davus finishes, he goes over to him.)

SMICRINES *(rolling his eyes heavenward and speaking in sepulchral tones)* This is an unexpected blow, Davus.
DAVUS A terrible one.

SMICRINES   How did it happen? How did he die?

DAVUS   (*shrugging despondently*)   What's hard for a
soldier to find is the chance to stay alive; chances to die
are all around.

SMICRINES   (*insistently*)   Tell me what happened anyway, Davus.

DAVUS   There's a river in Lycia called the Xanthus. We
fought a good number of battles there, and our side had
done well: the enemy had left the plain and fled. (*Ruefully*)
But I gess not being a great success also has its useful side
—the man who slips a bit is put on his guard. A devil-
may-care attitude left us in total disorder for what was
to come. A lot of the men, you see, left the camp and went
off sacking villages, ravaging the fields, selling off booty;
everyone came back with quite a haul.

SMICRINES   Not bad!

DAVUS   Cleostratus put together a shipment of some six
hundred gold pieces, quite a lot of plate, and the batch
of prisoners you see over there, and sends me off to
Rhodes with instructions to leave it all with some friend
and come right back.

SMICRINES   Well, what happened?

DAVUS   I set out at dawn. The day I left, the enemy,
managing to sneak past the men we had on watch, was lying
in wait, screened by a hill; they had learned from some
deserters how disorganized our forces were. When it got
dark, the men left the countryside with its rich pickings
and all disappeared into the tents. Then, as will happen,
most of them got good and drunk.

SMICRINES   (*shaking his head*)   Bad, very bad.

DAVUS   Yes, since the enemy, I gather, made a sudden
attack . . . [About three and a half lines are lost here.]
Round about midnight I'm standing guard over the money
and the captives, walking up and down in front of my
tent, when I hear shouts, groans, wailing, running, men
calling out to each other. And from them I heard what
had happened. Luckily, where we were there was a small
ridge that made a good strongpoint. We all gathered on top
of it, and wounded men from the various units kept pour-
ing in.

SMICRINES   Lucky thing for you Cleostratus had sent
you off when he did.

DAVUS   At dawn we went about pitching a sort of camp
there and stayed put, while the men who had gone off on
the forays I told you about kept blaming themselves for
our troubles. On the fourth day we found out that the
enemy was off taking their prisoners to the villages inland,
so we marched out.

SMICRINES   And he had fallen and you saw him among
the dead?

DAVUS   I wasn't able to identify him for sure. After four
days of lying there, the faces were all swollen.

SMICRINES   Then how do you know?

DAVUS   (*holding out the shield he has been clutching*)
He was lying there with his shield. It was all bashed in—
I suppose that's why none of the enemy bothered to take
it. (*Bitterly*) That fine commanding officer of ours didn't
let us gather the bones and hold a funeral for each one,
because he saw it would take too much time, but had us
collect the corpses and hold a mass cremation. Then he had
us carry out a quick burial and break camp right away.
We first made it safely to Rhodes and, after staying there
a few days, sailed here. (*Shrugging despondently*) That's
my whole story.

SMICRINES   (*being elaborately casual*)   You say you
have six hundred gold pieces?

DAVUS   That's right.

SMICRINES   And plate?

DAVUS   About forty pounds of it. (*Noting Smicrines' face
fall*)   No more than that, Mr. Legal Heir.

SMICRINES   (*in a perish-the-thought tone*)   What do you
mean? You think that's the reason I'm asking? Good
heavens! (*Unable to restrain his curiosity*) The enemy
get the rest?

DAVUS   (*nodding gloomily*)   Just about the best part
of it, except for what I got away with before the trouble
started. (*Pointing to the bundles some of the captives are
carrying*) There are coats and cloaks in there. (*Gesturing
toward the whole group of captives*) And this bunch you
see here is his property.

SMICRINES   (*holding his hand to his eyes, sepulchrally*)
All this doesn't mean a thing to me. If only he had lived!
DAVUS   If only! (*Sighing*)   Let's go in and tell the sad
news to the last people in the world we should bring
such news.
SMICRINES   I'll want to have a little chat with you soon,
Davus, when we're not so pressed. Right now, I think I
should go inside too and think over what's the kindest way
to handle them.

(*Smicrines goes into his house, and Davus, followed by the
file of captives, enters Chaerestratus' house, where Cleostratus' sister has been staying since her brother left. As soon
as the stage is empty, a woman dressed in impressive robes
enters. Representing Lady Luck, she delivers the Prologue.*)

LADY LUCK   Now if something had happened to them
(*indicating by a gesture Davus and Chaerestratus' household*)   that actually involved tragedy, it would hardly be
fitting for me, a goddess, to be following right on their
heels. At this moment, however, they're in the dark, they're
floundering about. [About three lines are lost here.] The
enemy attacked, the trumpets blew the alarm without
stopping, and everybody ran to the rescue, grabbing whatever arms were near at hand. That's how the man who happened to be alongside Cleostratus ran out with the shield
you saw. A few minutes later he had fallen. With the
shield lying there among the corpses and the man's face
all swollen, Davus mistook him for his master. Cleostratus,
who had run out with someone else's armor, ended up a
prisoner of war. He's alive and will appear pretty soon,
safe and sound.
    All right, you know all you need to on that score. Let's
turn to the old man who was asking all those questions
just now. In family, he's Cleostratus' uncle on the father's
side; in nastiness, he's the world's worst. He doesn't recognize friend or relative, there isn't a foul trick in life he'd
stop at, he's out to get his hands on everything—this is
all he knows. He lives by himself with an old woman as
housekeeper. The house next door, the one Cleostratus'

servant just went into, is where this old miser's younger
brother lives. He's also an uncle of Cleostratus', but he's
a fine person who lives well and has a wife and one daughter.
When Cleostratus sailed off, he left his sister in this man's
care; the two girls have been brought up like foster sisters.
This younger uncle, being, as I mentioned, a fine person
and realizing that Cleostratus would be away a rather long
time and that the young fellow's means were very moderate,
was going to arrange a marriage himself for the girl to
his stepson, his wife's child by a former husband, and he
was going to give her a gift of $60,000 to serve as dowry.
Matter of fact, he was going to hold the wedding right
now, but this blow that has just fallen will upset things
for all of them. The old rascal, you see, having heard a
minute ago about the six hundred gold pieces and having
gotten a look at the captives and the load of baggage and
the slave girls, is going to want to get the girl for himself
now that she's an heiress, even though he's so old. But,
after putting himself to a lot of toil and trouble for nothing,
and after making perfectly clear to everybody just what
kind of person he is, he's going to wind up exactly where
he started.

Well, the only thing left for me to do is tell you who
I am. I am the one in charge of deciding and arranging
all these matters—I am Lady Luck.

(*The door of Smicrines' house opens, and Smicrines comes
out. He walks downstage and addresses the audience.*)

SMICRINES   Just so no one would call me a money-mad
miser, I showed I was perfectly willing to let everything
be carried inside without any check on how much gold and
plate there was, without any counting of anything. You
see, every time they can, they say nasty things about me.
(*Grinning craftily*)   Just so long as the carrying is done
by the family servants, I'll get an exact inventory. (*After
a moment's reflection*) I imagine they're willing to stand
by what's right and proper, but if they're not, they won't
get away with it. And this wedding that's to take place—
I want to tell them not to hold it. (*After another moment*

of reflection) But maybe it's stupid even to mention it. No one does any marrying when news of this sort comes along. Anyway, I'll knock on the door and call Davus out. He's the only one who'll pay me some attention.

(*At this moment Davus appears in the doorway of Chaerestratus' house.*)

DAVUS   (*through the doorway to the womenfolk inside*) Your reacting this way is completely understandable. But you must do the best you can under the circumstances to bear this misfortune like sensible people.

(*As he starts going off, stage right, Smicrines calls to him.*)

SMICRINES   I'm here to see you, Davus.
DAVUS   Me?
SMICRINES   Yes, you. (*Coming up to Davus, and raising his eyes to heaven*) If only he were alive, as he so deserved to be, not only to arrange these matters but to become master of all my possessions when I die, as the law provides!
DAVUS   If only. (*Eyeing him keenly*) What's on your mind?
SMICRINES   On my mind? I'm the elder. And, though my brother does me wrong and I see him constantly taking a bigger share than mine, I put up with it.
DAVUS   Very wise of you.
SMICRINES   But, my dear fellow, he doesn't know there's a limit! What's he think I am, a cheap slave? an illegitimate member of the family? Because just now he was going ahead with a wedding, giving the girl to some nobody without taking it up with me, without asking me—and I'm as much her uncle as he is.
DAVUS   Well, what about it?
SMICRINES   Seeing all these things makes me mad. Since he's acting like a stranger towards me, this is what I'm going to do. I'm not going to abandon property that's mine

to them to tear into shreds. *I'm* going to marry that girl,
just as some of the people I know are advising me to do.
(*Giving him an arch look*)   As a matter of fact, Davus,
I have the impression the law says something to that
effect.[1] Now you've got to figure out with me the right
way to do this. You're one of the family.

DAVUS   And I, Smicrines, have the strong impression that
that saying "Know thyself" is one people have thought
about a good deal. Let me follow it. Bring to me any matter
that should be brought before an honest servant, look to
me for discussion of these things . . . [about five and a half
lines are lost here.] I can talk about what dealings Cleostratus had while he was abroad. If I'm ordered, I'll de-
scribe them one by one, where, how, in whose presence.
But, god in heaven, when it comes to estates or heiresses,
Smicrines, and marriage and family and how people are
related—please, all of you, don't drag Davus into the middle.
What doesn't involve slaves, you people take care of your-
selves; that sort of thing will be in your line.

SMICRINES   (*snarling*)   Damn it all, you thing I'm making a mistake, eh?

DAVUS   (*diplomatically*)   I come from Phrygia. Lots of
the things you people think are so good seem just the
opposite to me, seem terrible. But what's the good of
taking up anything with me? Your ideas are better than
any of mine, naturally.

SMICRINES   (*looking him in the eye*)   I gather what
you're telling me now is, more or less, "Don't give me any
trouble," that sort of thing. I understand. (*Thinking a
moment, then gesturing towards Chaerestratus' house*)   I'll
have to go downtown and see one of them there, if there's
nobody home now.

DAVUS   (*quickly*)   Not a soul. (*Smicrines shrugs, turns,
and goes off, stage left. Davus raises his eyes to heaven.*)
Lady Luck, after a master like the one I lost, you're going
to turn me over to one like this? What did I do wrong to
you that was so terrible!

---

[1] Smicrines indeed did have the law on his side. In Athens in Menander's day, an heiress could be claimed by the nearest of kin, beginning
with the uncles on the father's side.

(The door of Chaerestratus' house opens, and a cook comes out followed by an assistant loaded down with pots, pans, dishware, and the like. The cook stops in front of the door, and his assistant with a sigh of relief puts his burden down.)

COOK   *(to the world at large)*   Even if I do get a job, either someone dies and then I have to get out in a hurry with no pay, or one of the girls in the house who's been pregnant with no one knowing it has her baby, and then suddenly they don't want a party any longer, and I'm out of the house and gone. *(Shaking his head dismally)* Of all the luck!

DAVUS   For god's sake, cook, on your way!

COOK   *(grumbling)*   What do you think I'm doing right now? *(To the assistant)* Pick up the knives! And make it snappy! *(To the world at large)* After ten days without work, I get a job that pays fifteen dollars. I figure I have the money sewed up. And along comes some corpse from Lycia and grabs this money right out of my hand. *(Noticing that the assistant is carrying a wine jug that is empty)* You godforsaken good-for-nothing! Trouble like this hits a household and you see the women busy wailing and tearing their hair—and you come out without filling up your jug! You don't let chances like this go by, you hear! *(To himself, grumbling)* Some servant I have here. What's he think his name is anyway, Diogenes? *(To the offender)* I can see you doing without dinner tonight. *(To the world at large)* And that waiter of mine—I suppose he's waiting to be invited to the funeral banquet.

(At this moment the gentleman in question appears in the doorway.)

WAITER   *(through the doorway to those inside)*   If I don't get my five dollars, I'll be tearing my hair myself, just like all of you.

DAVUS   *(to the cook, gesturing toward the waiter)* Come on. Don't you see him? *(The two walk up to the doorway.)*

[Three lines are lost here. Apparently the waiter asked Davus whether it really was true that he had brought a fortune in gold and silver and captives safely home.]

DAVUS   Absolutely.

WAITER   Then goddamn you to hell for doing a thing like that! Are you out of your mind? All that gold and those slaves, and you brought it back and didn't clear out? Where are you from, anyway?

DAVUS   (*stiffly*) We Phrygians—

WAITER   (*interrupting scornfully*) Are nothing to rave about, a bunch of fags. (*Thumping his chest*) Take us Thracians now. We're the only real men left. And us fellows from east Thrace—one hundred percent man, by god! (*Grinning*) That's why the jails are full of us.

DAVUS   Away from the door and on your way. (*Looking towards the exit, stage right*) Matter of fact, I see some other gang of men heading this way, those there, and they're drunk. (*The cook and his team exit, stage left, and a chorus—"the other gang of men"—enters, stage right. Davus calls out to them.*) Very smart of you. You never can tell what's going to happen; enjoy yourself as long as you can!

(*Davus goes into Chaerestratus' house. The chorus dances an entr'acte.*)

ACT II

(*Smicrines, Chaerestratus, and Chaereas enter, stage left, deep in conversation. Chaerestratus, though not much younger than Smicrines, looks a dozen years his junior, and his frank open face, courtly manner, and expensive and tasteful clothes make the contrast with his brother almost total. Chaereas is an agreeable, handsome young fellow, dressed as a rich man's son would be, yet without ostentation. During the whole scene he stands by his foster-father in tight-lipped silence.*)

SMICRINES   (*curtly*)   Very good, very good. And now what are you saying, Chaerestratus?

CHAERESTRATUS   First of all, my dear fellow, we have to get busy on the tomb.

SMICRINES   (*as before*)   We'll get busy right away. Next point—don't promise the girl to anyone. It's my affair, not yours; I'm the elder. You've got a wife, a daughter; I've still to get them.

CHAERESTRATUS   (*astonished*)   Smicrines! Have you lost your sense of proportion?

SMICRINES   (*sharply*)   Hey there! Why do you say that?

CHAERESTRATUS   You're going to marry a young girl? At your age?

SMICRINES   (*acting puzzled*)   What age?

CHAERESTRATUS   To me you are—no question about it—an old man.

SMICRINES   (*truculently*)   Am I the only oldster who's ever gotten married?

CHAERESTRATUS   (*nervously and rapidly*)   Smicrines, in god's name, take what's happened like a man. Chaereas here, who is going to marry her, was brought up with the girl. (*Frantically*) Let me say this: don't you lose a thing by it—take whatever there is, every bit of it, for yourself; you take possession of it, we give it to you. But let that poor little girl get a boy her own age to marry. And I'll take care of the dowry out of my own pocket; I'll give her $60,000.

SMICRINES   (*snarling*)   God in heaven, you think you're talking with some dumb hick? What are you saying? I should take the property and leave the girl to him (*gesturing contemptuously toward Chaereas*) so that, when they have a baby, I get sued for taking what belongs to the child?

CHAERESTRATUS   (*shocked*)   Is that what you think? Get it out of your mind!

SMICRINES   (*scornfully*)   "Think", you say? (*Between his teeth*) I want you people to send Davus to me to make me up an inventory of everything he's brought.

CHAERESTRATUS   Why must. . . [Half a line is lost here.] What should I have done?

[Smicrines' reply, a line or so long, is lost. At the end of it, he turns on his heel and goes into his house.]

CHAERESTRATUS   (*to Chaereas*)   My idea was that, with you marrying my niece and Cleostratus my daughter, I would leave you two in possession of all my worldly goods. (*Frantically*) May I leave this world this minute before I see what I never in my life expected to! (*He rushes into his house.*)

CHAEREAS   (*to himself, bitterly*)   That's fine. (*Apostrophizing Cleostratus*) Cleostratus, it stands to reason, I suppose, that your tragedy has first call on our pity and tears. But mine comes right after yours! (*Gesturing towards Chaerestratus' house*) None of these people have been hit as hard as I have. I fell in love, helplessly in love, with your sister—the sister of my dearest friend. I didn't take advantage of her, I did nothing to be ashamed of, nothing wrong. I followed the rules and asked for her hand in marriage from your uncle, with whom you had left her, and my mother, by whom she's being brought up, and I thought my life was just about bliss. But after all my thoughts of having arrived at the perfect life, after all my expectations, I'm not even going to be able to see her any more; the law throws out my claim and puts her in the hands of someone else.

(*As Chaereas falls silent, the door of Chaerestratus' house opens, and Davus and Chaerestratus appear. Davus is pulling his companion by main force out of the door.*)

DAVUS   (*earnestly*)   Chaerestratus, this is no way to do things. Get hold of yourself! You can't just lie down and give up hope. (*Noticing Chaereas and calling*) Chaereas, come over here; you talk to him. Don't let him be this way. What happens to every single one of us depends on him, just about. (*To Chaerestratus*) No, you must keep

open house. Show yourself in public. Chaerestratus, are
you going to abandon your friends in this chicken-hearted
way?

CHAERESTRATUS   (*wildly*)   Davus, I'm in a bad way!
What's happened is turning me into a manic depressive. I
swear to god, I'm not in my right mind, I'm on the point
of going mad. This is the state I'm in, thanks to the dirty
dealings of that fine brother of mine. You know what? He's
going to marry her himself!

DAVUS   (*aghast*)   What's that you say? Marry her?
But will he be able to?

CHAERESTRATUS   (*bitterly*)   That's what the hon-
orable gentleman says. And I'm even giving him every
single thing Cleostratus sent back!

DAVUS   (*shaking his head grimly*)   They don't make
them filthier.

CHAERESTRATUS   Filth, that's what he is. (*Wildly*)
So help me, I'm not going to stay alive if I'm to see this
happen!

DAVUS   (*thoughtfully*)   How could anyone get the better
of a dirty crook like that?

CHAERESTRATUS   A tough job.

DAVUS   (*with sudden animation*)   A tough job—but it
can be done!

CHAERESTRATUS   Can be done? By god, it's sure worth
fighting for.

DAVUS   So help me, if someone's rushed into . . . [about
six lines are lost here.] . . . you'll see someone who's rashly
made a mistake, and you'll handle him easily. Because,
with his eyes and mind fixed only on what he's after, he'll
be the worst possible judge of what's true or false.

CHAERESTRATUS   What are you driving at? Because
I'm ready to do whatever you want.

DAVUS   (*bringing the two close to him, conspiratorially*)
You people have to play roles in another tragedy—but of
a different kind. (*To Chaerestratus*) What you were talking about a minute ago—now you've got to make it seem
to happen. That you sort of lost all hope because of the
tragedy of Cleostratus' death, and the tragedy of the girl
being given away in marriage, and because you see Chae-

reas here, who is like a son to you, in the depths of despair. You were hit with one or the other of such troubles. Most of the times that any of us get sick, grief is more or less involved. Besides, he knows very well that you naturally take things hard and tend to get depressed. Then we call in some doctor who'll give a learned discourse and say it's a case of inflammation of the lungs, or inflammation of the brain, or some other deadly disease.

CHAERESTRATUS   And then what?

DAVUS   You suddenly die. We wail, "Poor Chaerestratus! Gone forever!" And we tear our hair in front of the door. You'll be locked away inside, and a dummy of your corpse, all wrapped up, will be laid out for all to see.

CHAERESTRATUS   (*to Chaereas, blankly*)   Do you get what he's driving at?

CHAEREAS   (*to Chaerestratus*)   Darned if I do.

CHAERESTRATUS   (*to Chaereas*)   Neither do I.

DAVUS   (*patiently*)   Your daughter, in her turn, becomes an heiress, just like your niece right now. But your estate is about $1,800,000 while your niece has only $120,-000, and the old miser is the nearest relative of both of them.

CHAERESTRATUS   (*interrupting, excitedly*)   Now I get it!

DAVUS   Unless your head is as hard as rock. Well, he'll quickly and happily turn the one girl over, in front of three thousand witnesses, to the first man who asks for her, and he'll grab the other—

CHAERESTRATUS   (*interrupting*)   That's what he'll think—and will he be sorry!

DAVUS   (*disregarding the interruption*)   —and he'll set about closing up the whole house, he'll lock the doors and put his seal on them, he'll be a millionaire—in his dreams.

CHAERESTRATUS   What about my dummy corpse?

DAVUS   It'll be laid out, and we'll all sit around in a circle, keeping an eye on him so he doesn't come near . . . [about eight lines are lost here].

CHAERESTRATUS   What you say, Davus, is all right with me. It suits me fine. What sweeter revenge on the old crook could you possibly think of?

DAVUS   (*between his teeth*)   By god, I'll make him pay
for every time he's ever hurt you. It's true what they say:
"A wolf with his mouth open goes off with his belly empty."
But we've got to get going right away. (*To Chaereas*) Chae-
reas, do you happen to know a doctor who's a foreigner?
A canny type, bit of a quack?
CHAEREAS   (*shaking his head*)   God no, not a soul.
DAVUS   Well, we have to have one.
CHAEREAS   (*brightening up*)   How about this? I go
and get one of my friends, and I ask around for a wig and
a long coat and a stick for him, and he puts on an accent
the best he can?
DAVUS   (*nodding assent vigorously*) But hurry!
CHAERESTRATUS   And what do I do?
DAVUS   What we've planned. To your death bed, and
god be with you!
CHAERESTRATUS   Right.
DAVUS   (*to the two of them*)   Don't let a word out.
Keep this matter to yourself, like men.
CHAEREAS   Who'll be in on it besides us?
CHAERESTRATUS   The only ones we have to tell are
my wife and the two girls, so they don't cry their eyes
out. We'll have to let the others think I'm dead and curse
me out all they want.
CHAEREAS   You're right. (*To Davus, gesturing towards
Chaerestratus*)   Have someone carry him inside. (*Grinning*) He'll have a fine time—and his worries whether the
disease will get started and the doctor can make a convincing case for us.

(*Davus and Chaerestratus go into the latter's house, with
Davus calling for a servant to come and help; Chaereas dashes
off, stage left. The stage is now empty, and the chorus comes
out and dances an entr'acte.*)

ACT III

(*The door of Smicrines' house opens, and Smicrines comes
out. He walks downstage and addresses the audience.*)

SMICRINES   (*bitterly*)   Davus sure came to me in a hurry with the inventory. Been very considerate about me, I must say! He's on their side. (*Snarling*) Well, by god, that's just fine; I'm grateful to him. I'm delighted to have a reason to go against him, to cross-examine him about these things the way *I* like and not have to do it friendly-like any longer. Because what we see is only half of what he brought back, no question about it. I know the tricks of that swindling slave!

(*The door of Chaerestratus' house flies open, and Davus bursts out.*)

DAVUS   (*at the top of his lungs to the world at large*)   Ye gods in heaven, I swear what just happened is frightening! I never dreamed such a terrible disease could hit a man that quickly! A bolt of fiery lightening has struck our house!
SMICRINES   (*to himself*)   What in the world does he mean?

[About four lines are lost here, in which Smicrines asks Davus what has happened, and the latter replies by spouting well-known quotations.[1]]
DAVUS

"Lives not the mortal who fore'er is blessed."

(*To himself*) Well done again, Davus! (*To the world at large*) Oh, my god in heaven, whoever expected this to happen! (*Starts running off, stage left.*)

---

[1] All but two come from lost tragedies; however, since they belong to the stock of Greek familiar quotations, most have been quoted by other writers and hence are known to us. Thus, "Lives not etc." comes from Euripides' *Stheneboea*, " 'Tis chance etc." from a play by Chaeremon, "When God etc." from Aeschylus' *Niobe*, "For so God's will" from some unknown play by Euripides. "The world holds etc." are the opening two lines of Euripides' *Orestes*, and "No easy thing" is line 232 of the same play. "Terrible beyond etc.", "In the list etc.", and "For God can etc." are unknown.

SMICRINES   (*calling*)   Damn you, Davus, where are you
running to?

DAVUS   (*stopping, to the world at large*)   Then there's
this:

> " 'Tis chance and not the well-laid plan
> That rules the doings of every man."

(*To himself*) Terrific! (*To the world at large*)

> "When God has willed to bring a house to shame,
> He sees to it we mortals bear the blame."

The noble Aeschylus—

SMICRINES   (*interrupting*)   So you're spouting prov-
erbs, you good-for-nothing?

DAVUS   (*disregarding him, to the world at large*)

> "Terrible beyond belief or thought—

SMICRINES   (*interrupting*)   Will you stop it!

DAVUS

> "In the list of human grief
> Is there any past belief?"

as Carcinus puts it.

> "For God can bring in a day's short span
> The blight of sorrow to the happiest man."

Well said, all of them, Smicrines.

SMICRINES   (*exasperated*)   What are you talking
about?

DAVUS   (*lugubriously*)   Your brother—oh god, how
shall I say it?—is on the point of death.

SMICRINES   (*genuinely astonished*)   My brother—who
was talking to me on this very spot just a minute ago?
What's the matter?

DAVUS   (*throwing up his hands in despair*)   Bile, de-
pression, mental derangement, loss of breath.
SMICRINES   My God! Some dread disease!
DAVUS

> "There's naught we can call so dread,
> no fell disease—"

SMICRINES   (*interrupting*)   You give me a pain.
DAVUS

> "For so God's will has ever been:
> That blows of fate come unforeseen."

(*Resentfully*)   The first's from Euripides, the second from
Chaeremon. I don't quote second-raters.
SMICRINES   Has a doctor come?
DAVUS   No. But Chaereas has gone to get one.
SMICRINES   (*eyeing him narrowly*)   And who, I'd like
to know?
DAVUS   (*suddenly looking stage left and pointing*)   By
god, it looks as if it's that one there. (*Calling*)   Please!
Hurry!

(*The Doctor, with an assistant at his heels, enters, stage
left, and paces across the stage in a slow pompous strut.
Davus rushes over and starts hurrying him along.*)

DAVUS   (*as he hustles them into the house*)

> "No easy thing it is to please
> The helpless victims of disease."

SMICRINES   (*starting to follow them into the house,
and then stopping; to the audience*)   If they see me, they'll
say I came right away because I was glad, I know darned
well they will. And my brother won't be overjoyed to
see me.

[About sixteen lines are lost here, in which Smicrines continues his soliloquy while the "doctor" presumably carries on his examination inside the house. The minute he comes out, Smicrines begins quizzing him, and the text resumes at some point during this dialogue. Much of it is fragmentary, but the sense can be followed.]

DOCTOR   . . . und der bile . . . und diss iss because of hiss present veak condition.

SMICRINES   . . . this, of course, I understand.

DOCTOR   . . .

SMICRINES   These matters, of course, I understand.

DOCTOR   My opinion iss dat hiss mind hass [been affected] . . . A case of vat ve doctors call inflammation of der brain.

SMICRINES   I understand. But what about it? Is there no hope of recovery?

DOCTOR   If you vant der truth, cases like diss are critical.

SMICRINES   Don't spare me. I want the truth.

DOCTOR   It is absolute out of der question diss man can stay alife. He iss vomiting der bile. Der iss obscuring [of his vision] . . . und in de eyes . . . foams at der mouth und . . . . he hass der look of a corpse. . . . (*To his assistant*) Come, ve go. (*Starts to walk off, stage left.*)

SMICRINES   (*calling*)   Hey, you! You there!

DOCTOR   (*stopping and turning*) . . . you call me back?

SMICRINES   I certainly did . . . [Come] here. Further away from the door . . .

DOCTOR   . . . not shtay alife as before . . .

SMICRINES   . . . pray that in some way . . . lots of things happen . . .

DOCTOR   Go on, laugh . . . my knowlitch of medicine . . . und you look [sick] to me yourself . . . you're getting a case of tuberculosis. You heff eggzackly the look of a dead man. (*Exits, stage left.*)

SMICRINES   (*to himself*)   I can imagine the womenfolk carrying on over him as if he had died on the field of battle. And orders being shouted to the neighbors through the drainpipes.

(*Davus comes out of Chaerestratus' house.*)

DAVUS   (*to the audience, gesturing towards Smicrines*)
I'm going to set him on his ear. But what I did . . .

[The rest of the play is almost completely lost. All that is
left are some fragments of lines that provide a few clues.
    Davus and Chaereas very likely put on a lugubrious show
of grief and then went about whetting the old man's appetite
for the new heiress as a bride.
    Toward the end of Act IV, Cleostratus finally makes his ap-
pearance. Enough is preserved to reconstruct the scene of
his return. It begins with his entering, unrecognizable in his
torn and travel-worn clothes, and delivering a soliloquy, about
eight lines long, welcoming the sight of his homeland.]

CLEOSTRATUS   (*as he ends his soliloquy*)   I must knock
    on the door.
DAVUS   (*as he opens the door*)   [Who is it?]
CLEOSTRATUS   Me.
DAVUS   (*not recognizing him*)   Who do you want? The
    owner of this house has died. . .
CLEOSTRATUS   (*aghast*)   Died! Oh, god. . .
DAVUS   . . . and please don't bother people who are in
    mourning. . .
CLEOSTRATUS   Oh my god, my god! My poor poor
    uncle. . .
DAVUS   God god! Mister, . . .
CLEOSTRATUS   Davus! What are you saying? . . .
DAVUS   . . . I have you!

[In the dozen lines that follow to the end of Act IV, Davus
must have acquainted Cleostratus with the true state of
affairs.
    In the fifth and last act, Chaerestratus was no doubt hastily
resurrected, Cleostratus welcomed by the rest of the family,
and Smicrines completely unmasked in a confrontation with
two souls apparently returned from the grave. A fragmentary line mentions a "double marriage"; the play, then, probably ended with Chaereas marrying Cleostratus' sister, and
Cleostratus Chaerestratus' daughter.]

The Arbitration

DRAMATIS PERSONAE

SMICRINES, an elderly, well-to-do Athenian, father of Pamphila and father-in-law of Charisius
CHAERESTRATUS, a friend and neighbor of Charisius
SYRISCUS, a charcoal burner, slave of Chaerestratus
DAVUS, a goatherd (slave)
ONESIMUS, Charisius' valet (slave)
HABROTONON, a young professional entertainer (slave), hired by Charisius
PAMPHILA, daughter of Smicrines and wife of Charisius
CHARISIUS, a young, well-to-do Athenian, recently married to Pamphila
SOPHRONA, Pamphila's old nurse

SCENE

A street on the outskirts of Athens. Two houses front on it, Chaerestratus' and Charisius'. The exit on stage left leads downtown, that on stage right to the open country.

ACT I

[Less than a quarter of this act is preserved. The loss is not so serious as it might appear since a large part of the act was given over to introducing the characters and conveying to

the audience the information it had to have in order to follow
the action, and most of this can be deduced from the surviving
portions. Probably the exposition was made through an ini-
tial scene in dialogue between several of the minor characters,
followed by a formal statement by an actor playing the role
of Prologue.

What the audience learned was this: Charisius had married Pamphila five months ago. Four months before the wedding, at the festival to Artemis called the Tauropolia, an all-
woman festival that was held at night, a drunken youth had
crashed the affair and attacked her; in the struggle she had
somehow managed to grab his ring but, in the darkness, had
had no chance to see his face. As will happen in the world of
the theater, whether that of the Greek comic stage or of Hol-
lywood, she became pregnant. Luckily, soon after the wedding,
her husband left on an extended trip and she was able to keep
her condition a secret; and he was still away when her baby
was born. Since she loved Charisius deeply and didn't want
to run any risk of spoiling her newly launched marriage, she
took advantage of his absence to get rid of the child. She
swaddled him up, tied to him a packet containing the ring
and a few other distinctive bits of jewelry—"birth tokens"
as the Greeks called them—and, helped by her old nurse,
smuggled the pathetic bundle out of the house and left it in
some brush on a nearby hillside. It was her misfortune, however, that in some way Charisius' valet, Onesimus, got wind
of what was going on and, when Charisius returned, in-
formed him that the wife he was convinced was so innocent
and chaste had just gotten rid of an illegitimate child. Charisius, who was a thoroughgoing prig, a holier-than-thou sort,
decided then and there to end the marriage. But he was un-
willing to initiate proceedings and submit her to public scandal
and himself to public ridicule; instead he did what is done
so often today: he set about giving her open-and-shut grounds
for divorcing him. He moved into his friend Chaerestratus'
house next door. He began to throw money around right and
left on a series of around-the-clock wild parties. He even hired
a professional entertainer, Habrotonon, as his mistress. The
pose, of course, was not easy for him to maintain since conduct of this kind was uncharacteristic.

Pamphila, though alone in Charisius' house and utterly miserable, was determined to stick it out in the vague hope that all would somehow work out. But not her father, Smicrines. This crusty old businessman, the kind who goes through life getting full value for every cent spent, was horrified by the stories he was hearing of his new son-in-law's extravagance. Concerned about the dowry he had provided, as well as about his daughter (he, of course, knew nothing about her child), he came to visit her. The first scene we have preserved starts at this point.]

(Chaerestratus, Charisius' friend and neighbor, comes on stage from his house. As he does, Smicrines enters, stage left, grumbling to himself.)

SMICRINES   That man and his drinking! I'm downright shocked. I don't mean about his getting drunk. No, what's inconceivable to me is that anyone would drive himself to drink when it costs a dollar a glass!

CHAERESTRATUS   *(aside)*   I was expecting this. Once he breaks in on us, that's the end of our fun with the girls.

SMICRINES   *(to himself)*   Why should I care? He's the one who'll be sorry. But there's the dowry—he takes a hundred and twenty thousand dollars from me, and then doesn't even consider himself a part of his wife's household! Sleeps away from home. Even hires a mistress from a pimp. *(Throwing up his hands horrified)* At sixty dollars a day!

CHAERESTRATUS   *(aside)*   Sixty dollars? He knows everything down to the details.

SMICRINES   *(to himself)*   Enough to feed a man for a month. *(Making a mental calculation)* And six days besides.

CHAERESTRATUS   *(aside)*   He's got it all figured out— a dollar and a half a day, just enough to get you a bowl of soup if you're starving.

(One of the girls comes out of Chaerestratus' house and addresses him.)

GIRL   Chaerestratus, Charisius is waiting for you. *(Pointing to Smicrines)* Who is *that?*

CHAERESTRATUS   Pamphila's father.
GIRL   . . . he looks pretty miserable . . .

[Some fifteen lines are lost here. Apparently the girl innocently suggested they tell Smicrines that his son-in-law was now staying with Chaerestratus.]

CHAERESTRATUS   If you know what's good for you, you won't tell him.
GIRL   (*pouting*) But I want to.
CHAERESTRATUS   (*losing his temper*) Oh, go to the devil! Just try it. You'll be sorry.
SMICRINES   (*to himself*) I'm going inside now to find out exactly how things stand with my daughter. Then I'll figure out how to tackle him. (*Enters Charisius' house.*)
GIRL   Shall we tell Charisius he's here?
CHAERESTRATUS   We'd better. That old fox can ruin a household.
GIRL   (*still smarting under Chaerestratus' angry words*) There's quite a few I wish he would.
CHAERESTRATUS   Quite a few?
GIRL   That one, for example, next door. (*Points to Chaerestratus' house.*)
CHAERESTRATUS   Mine?
GIRL   Yes, yours! Let's go in and see Charisius.
CHAERESTRATUS   Let's. (*Looking toward the wings*) As a matter of fact, a bunch of youngsters are coming this way and they're a little tight—this is no time to run into any trouble with them. (*Hurries her off into the house.*)

(*The stage is now empty, and a chorus comes on—the "bunch of youngsters"—and dances an entr'acte.*)

ACT II

(*Smicrines comes out of Charisius' house He hasn't accomplished very much: Charisius, of course, was not in the house, and his daughter, hugging the hope that time is somehow on her side, refuses to go along with his plans. As he walks slowly, buried in thought, away from the entrance, two slaves, Davus and Syriscus, enter stage right, arguing. Behind them is Syriscus' wife, holding an infant. Davus, a goatherd, is shrewd, has a keen eye for what's best for himself, and doesn't waste words. Syricus, a charcoal burner, is almost the exact opposite: open, absolutely honest, somewhat scatterbrained, and richly endowed with the gift of gab.*

Their argument is about the infant the woman is carrying and it has reached an impasse.)

SYRISCUS   (*heatedly*)   You're evading justice.

DAVUS   (*angrily*)   Damn you, that's a lie! I don't have to give you what's not yours.

SYRISCUS   Then we'll have to have somebody arbitrate the matter.

DAVUS   I'm willing. Let's arbitrate it.

SYRISCUS   But who?

DAVUS   Anyone will do for me. (*Disgustedly*)   I'm getting what I deserve. Why did I ever let you in on the deal?

SYRISCUS   (*pointing to Smicrines*)   Are you willing to take him as judge?

DAVUS   I'll risk it.

SYRISCUS   (*going up to Smicrines*)   I beg your pardon, could you spare us a minute of your time?

SMICRINES   (*jolted out of his thoughts*)   You? What about?

SYRISCUS   (*pointing to Davus*)   He and I have a little disagreement.

SMICRINES   (*impatiently*)   What's that got to do with me?

SYRISCUS   We're looking for somebody to arbitrate it, somebody impartial. If you have the time, would you please settle it for us?

SMICRINES   (*testily*)   Go to the devil! What is this— workmen in overalls going around arguing lawsuits?

SYRISCUS   (*unabashed*)   What if we do. It's a simple matter and won't take long to explain. Please do us the favor. And please don't think it's beneath you. (*Oratorically*)   Justice should triumph all the time, everywhere, and

whoever comes along should be concerned to do his part.
It's a duty we all share in life.

DAVUS   (*aside, sarcastically but a little worried*)   I've
got a real lawyer on my hands here! (*Shaking his head disgustedly*) Why did I ever let him in on the deal?

SMICRINES   (*curtly*)   Well, tell me, will you stand by
whatever I decide?

SYRISCUS   Absolutely.

SMICRINES   I'll hear the case. Why not? (*Turning to
Davus*) You there, you who aren't saying anything, you
speak first.

DAVUS   (*flatly, without wasting any words*)   I'll tell you
what went before too and not just what passed between
me and him, so you'll have the whole matter clear in your
mind. I was pasturing my flock in the brush near here
about a month ago, and, all by myself, I found an infant
that someone had abandoned. There was a necklace with
it and some pieces of jewelry like this. (*He shows some
trinkets.*)

SYRISCUS   (*breaking in*)   These are what we're arguing
about.

DAVUS   (*to Smicrines, angrily*)   He's not letting me
talk!

SMICRINES   (*turning to Syriscus*)   Don't interrupt or
I'll let you have it with this stick!

DAVUS   And serve him right.

SMICRINES   Keep talking.

DAVUS   I will. I picked up the baby and its things and
went home. I was going to raise it. At least, that was the
idea I had at the time. But, that night, just as happens to
everybody, I had second thoughts on the matter. I thrashed
it all out in my mind. What do I want the trouble of raising
a child for? Where would I get the money? What do I want
with such worries? That's how I felt. Next morning I went
out with my flock again. (*Gesturing toward Syriscus*)
This fellow came to the same place to cut out some stumps
—he's a charcoal burner. I had known him before, and we
got to talking. He saw I was down in the mouth, and says,
"What's on your mind, Davus?" "What's on my mind?" I

say. "That I don't mind my own business!" And I told him
what happened, how I found a baby and took it home. So,
then, before I could tell him the whole story, he begins
begging, keeps interrupting me with, "Davus, give me the
baby and heaven will reward you. You'll be lucky. You'll
get your freedom. I've got a wife," he tells me, "she lost a
baby in childbirth." (*Pointing to the woman*) There she is
over there; she's got the baby with her now.

SMICRINES   (*turning to Syricus*)   Did you beg him?

DAVUS   (*to Syriscus, sharply*)   How about it, Syriscus?

SYRISCUS   (*unabashed*)   I did.

DAVUS   He certainly did, the whole day long. He kept
pestering me and jabbering away at me, so finally I gave
in. I gave it to him. It was nothing but "bless you, bless
you," when he left. He even grabbed my hands and kept
kissing them.

SMICRINES   (*to Syriscus*)   Did you?

SYRISCUS   (*as before*)   I did.

DAVUS   He went away. Now he and his wife meet me,
and all of a sudden he claims he should get the things that
were with the baby—little things, some trash, nothing at all,
believe me—and says he's getting a raw deal because I
claim I should keep them, and won't give them up. What I
say is that he ought to be grateful for the share he begged
out of me. Just because I don't give him everything is no
reason why I have to submit to an investigation. Suppose
he had found the baby while he was walking along with
me, and it was a case of finders-sharers? He still would
have gotten only what was his share and I what was mine.
(*Turns to Syriscus, and his voice rises with indignation*)
But I found it all by myself! You weren't even there at
the time! (*Shaking his head incredulously*) And you think
you should keep everything and I should have nothing!
(*Falls silent for a moment, still shaking his head, then resumes, more calmly, again addressing Syriscus.*) Let's cut
it short. I gave you, of my own free will, something that
belongs to me. If you're satisfied, keep it. If you're not, if
you've changed your mind, just give it right back. Then
you do nobody any harm and nobody does you any. But
you just can't have everything. You can't take what I gave

you of my own free will and then squeeze the rest out of me. (*Turning back to Smicrines*) I've had my say.

SYRISCUS (*to Smicrines, a little timidly, since he's afraid of the stick if he talks out of turn*) Is he done?

SMICRINES Are you deaf? He's done.

SYRISCUS Thank you. That means it's my turn. (*With candor*) He found the baby all by himself, and everything he says is the absolute truth. It all happened that way. I don't deny it. I got the baby by begging him for it, on my knees. It's the truth. (*Pauses to let this sink in, then proceeds melodramatically*) I happened to learn from some shepherd he'd been chatting with, fellow who works for the same master, that he had also found some jewelry with the child. (*Adopting the pose and manner of a trial lawyer*) Your Honor, my client is here in person to claim this jewelry. (*To his wife*) Hand me the baby. (*Turning to Davus*) Davus, my client is here for his necklace and birth tokens. He claims that they were intended for his neck, not your pocket. And I'm representing him, since he's my ward. You made him so yourself, when you gave him to me. (*Hands the baby back to his wife and again addresses Smicrines*) Your Honor, as I see it, what you have to decide is whether this jewelry, gold or whatever it is, should be kept in escrow for the child until he grows up, in accordance with the will of the mother, whoever she was, or whether this baby-robber here should keep it, just because he was the first to find something that didn't belong to him. (*Turning to Davus*) You want to know why I didn't ask you for the jewelry when I got the baby? Because at that time I didn't yet have the right to speak in its behalf. And even now I'm not coming to ask for one single thing for myself. Finders-sharers? Don't talk of "finding" something when a party's been wronged. That isn't finding, it's stealing! (*Turning back to Smicrines*) And there's this to think about (*looking off into the distance, dreamily*): for all we know this child is above our station. Even though he's been brought up among working people, the time may come when he'll look down on our ways and show the stuff he's made of and go in for the sort of things gentlemen do—lion hunting, or an army career, or sports. (*Fac-

ing Smicrines again) I'm sure you've been to the theater and remember lots of situations like this. There's the one where an old goatherd, fellow who wore clothes the same as mine, found those heroes Neleus and Pelias. When he realized they were above his station, he told them the whole story, how he found them and brought them up, and he gave them a little bag full of their birth tokens, and, from that time on, having found out the truth about themselves, they were kings—the same fellows who had been goatherds up to then! But if a Davus had taken these tokens and sold them off to make himself fifty dollars, they would have gone through the rest of their days without ever knowing how high their station in life really was. What good is it for me to go ahead and raise the child if Davus is going to destroy the one hope of ever saving him? (*Carried away by his own eloquence, again gazing off into space, dreamily*) Why, once birth tokens saved a man from marrying his sister. Another time they helped a man find his mother and rescue her. Once they saved a brother. Life is full of pitfalls for every one of us. We've got to have foresight, we've got to be on the alert, we've got to look far ahead, as best we can. (*Pauses to recover from this verbal flight, and returns to the matter at hand.*) "Give it right back if you're not satisfied," he tells me, and he thinks he's got a strong point there. What's the justice in that? (*Turning to Davus*) You find you have to give up what belongs to the baby, so you're out to get your hands on the baby too—just so you can do your robbing all over again with no worries at all, seeing that Lady Luck intervened to keep the jewelry safe from you this time. (*To Smicrines*) I'm done now. Decide whatever you think is right.

SMICRINES   (*promptly*) It's simple. The baby keeps whatever was left with it. That's my decision.

DAVUS   Fine. But what about the baby?

SMICRINES   (*indignantly*) Good god, do you think I'd give it to you, the man who is out to cheat it? No! It goes to the man who came to the rescue and went after you when you tried to cheat it.

SYRISCUS   (*fervently*) God bless you!

DAVUS   (*outraged*) God almighty, what a hell of a decision! I found everything and I have to cough it all up; he found nothing and he gets everything. You mean I have to hand it all over?

SMICRINES   (*curtly*)   That's what I mean.

DAVUS   (*as before*)   What a hell of a decision! I'll be god damned!

SYRISCUS   Come on, let's have the stuff.

DAVUS   My god, what I have to put up with!

SYRISCUS   Open up that pouch and show us what's in it. I know you've got the stuff there. (*To Smicrines, who is starting to move off*) Please, wait just a second and make him hand the things over.

DAVUS   (*grumbling to himself*)   Why did I ever let him (*gesturing toward Smicrines*) handle the case?

SYRISCUS   Hand it over, you stinker!

DAVUS   (*handing the jewelry over*)   The dirty, lowdown treatment I have to put up with!

SMICRINES   (*to Syriscus*)   Have you got everything?

SYRISCUS   I think so; unless he swallowed something when I was arguing my case and he knew he was going to lose.

DAVUS   (*still dumbstruck, to himself*)   I wouldn't have believed it!

SYRISCUS   (*to Smicrines as he walks off, stage left*) Goodbye, and thanks! (*Admiringly*) All our judges ought to be like that.

DAVUS   (*to himself*)   A dirty deal, so help me. Never heard a worse decision in my life.

SYRISCUS   You were a crook.

DAVUS   Listen, you crook you, you better keep this stuff safe until that baby grows up, because, believe me, I'm going to keep an eye on you as long as I live.

SYRISCUS   On your way, on your way! (*Davus leaves, stage right, and Syriscus addresses his wife.*) Take all this and bring it inside to our master, Chaerestratus. Because we're going to spend the night here, pay what we owe, and then go back to work in the morning. But first let's check these things over, every one of them. Got a box? (*She shakes her head.*) Then spread out your skirt and put them there.

(*At this point Onesimus, Charisius' valet, comes out of Chaerestratus' house. He's nattily dressed, as one would expect of the personal attendant of a rich master. He rather prides himself on knowing his way around, on being a man of the world. He also likes to know everything that's going on, and has a flair for successful snooping—witness his learning of Pamphila's baby.*)

ONESIMUS   (*muttering to himself as he comes out of the door*) Never saw such a slow cook. By this time yesterday people were well into the after-dinner drinks.

SYRISCUS   (*to his wife as they examine the child's jewelry*) This looks like a rooster. (*With a grin*) Wouldn't try to eat it, though. Here, take it. Here's something with stones. And here's a little ax.

ONESIMUS   (*his curiosity piqued, looks over the pair's shoulders; then, to himself*) What's going on here?

SYRISCUS   (*as before*) Here's a gold-plated ring; it's iron underneath. It's got a seal: a bull or a goat, I can't make out which. "Made by Cleostratus" it says.

ONESIMUS   (*breaking in*) Let me see it.

SYRISCUS   (*absentmindedly*) Here. (*Suddenly realizing what he has done*) Hey, who are you?

ONESIMUS   (*goggling at the ring*) Just can't be!

SYRISCUS   Who can't be?

ONESIMUS   The ring.

SYRISCUS   (*testily*) What do you mean, ring? What are you talking about?

ONESIMUS   It's my master's ring! It's Charisius'!

SYRISCUS   You're out of your mind.

ONESIMUS   One that he lost.

SYRISCUS   (*reaching for the ring*) Damn you, give me that ring back!

ONESIMUS   (*holding it out of reach*) Give you our ring? Where did you get it, anyway?

SYRISCUS   (*indignantly, to himself*) God damn it, what the hell's going on here? What a job it is to keep a poor orphan's property safe! The minute someone comes along he's out to get his hands on it. (*To Onesimus*) You heard me! Give me that ring!

ONESIMUS   Are you kidding? God damn it, it belongs to my master!

SYRISCUS   (*with the jewelry still in his hands, decides to finish taking inventory before tackling Onesimus in earnest. Growling to himself*) He'll get any of this stuff over my dead body! I'll haul 'em into court, one after the other— my mind's made up. This stuff's the baby's, not mine. (*To his wife as he resumes the inventory*) Here, take this, it's some kind of necklace. And a piece of red cloth. Now go inside. (*She goes into Chaerestratus' house. He straightens up and turns to Onesimus*) Now, what's this you're telling me?

ONESIMUS   (*startled out of his fascinated study of the ring*) Who me? Oh, it belongs to Charisius. He got drunk once and lost it; at least that's what he said.

SYRISCUS   (*relieved to hear that the alleged owner is his master's best friend*) All right. I'm in Chaerestratus' household. Take good care of it, or give it back to me and I'll keep it safe for you.

ONESIMUS   (*hastily*) I don't mind taking care of it.

SYRISCUS   Makes no difference to me. Looks to me as if we're both headed for the same place (*pointing to Chaerestratus' house*).

ONESIMUS   Listen, there's a party going on now, and maybe it isn't a good time to tell him about all this. How about tomorrow?

SYRISCUS   (*grimly*) I'll be around. Tomorrow I'm ready to let anyone you want arbitrate the case. That's it in a nutshell. (*To himself, as he watches Onesimus go off into Chaerestratus' house*) I didn't come off so badly the last time. Looks like I'll have to stop everything else and start practicing law. Only way a man can keep anything nowadays. (*Follows Onesimus into the house*).

(*The stage is now empty, and the chorus re-appears to perform an entr'acte*).

ACT III

(*Onesimus emerges from Chaerestratus' house. It is apparent that something is very much on his mind.*)

ONESIMUS   (*to himself*)   Time and again I started to go up to Charisius to show him this ring. I was right at his side, we were face to face—and I just couldn't go through with it. Now I'm sorry about what I told him before. He's been saying too often for comfort: "You! You had to go and tell me these things! I hope to god you break your neck!" I only hope he doesn't make up with his wife. Then he'll get rid of me—I'm the one who told him all about her; I know too much. It's a good thing I held off just now from adding anything more to the mess. It could land me in trouble—too much for comfort.

(*Habrotonon, the entertainer that Charisius had hired, now appears at the doorway of Chaerestratus' house. Habrotonon is a slave, owned by a slave dealer who hires her out. She does not consciously rebel at her lot, but, like any slave, she dreams unremittingly of that remote yet possible moment when she may gain her freedom, and is ready to grasp at whatever promises to bring it even a mite closer. A girl in her walk of life must learn to use her wits to get along; Habrotonon has become adept at the art. She is no doubt hard—she could hardly be otherwise and get by—but still young and attractive enough to keep this from showing. Aware of her undeniable charms and with the professional's pride in her skill at her trade, she is understandably resentful when her services are contracted for and go unused—as is the case at the moment with her present employer.*
    She is leaving the house to get away from the unwelcome advances of some drunks. Her first words are addressed through the door to them.)

HABROTONON   Stop bothering me and let me go. Please!
(*She manages to wrench herself loose, and leaves the door-*

way, muttering to herself.)   I guess I've been making a fool of myself without realizing it. I thought he wanted me to make love to, but the way that man hates me—it's really something out of this world! My god, he won't even let me sit next to him at the table; I've got to be somewhere else.

ONESIMUS   (*to himself, staring gloomily at the ring in his hand*)   Maybe I should give it back to the fellow I got it from. (*Thinking for a moment*)   No, that'll get me nowhere.

HABROTONON   (*to herself*)   He's in a bad way. What's he throwing away all this money on me for? My god, I could enroll as a vestal virgin right now for all that's gone on between him and me. I've been sitting around for three days now, chaste as a bride in white, as the saying goes.

ONESIMUS   (*to himself*)   How in heaven, how could—

(*His soliloquy is interrupted by Syriscus, who suddenly rushes out from Chaerestratus' house.*)

SYRISCUS   (*excitedly, to himself*)   Where is he? I've been looking for him all over the house. (*Suddenly seeing Onesimus*)   Hey, mister, give me back that ring or else show it to the fellow you were going to. Let's get this settled. I've got to get going.

ONESIMUS   (*confidentially*)   Look, old man, here's the situation. This is my master's ring. It's Charisius', all right; I'm sure of it. But I simply can't bring myself to show it to him. You know, if I hand him this ring, I just about make him the father of the child it was left with.

SYRISCUS   Don't be silly. How?

ONESIMUS   He lost it at the Festival of Artemis, the one where the women celebrate all night. It stands to reason that there was an attack on some girl, and then she had this baby and abandoned it. That's what must have happened. Now, if we could only find *her* and produce this ring, we'd be getting somewhere. But as things stand now, we'd only be getting people suspicious and upset.

SYRISCUS   (*not able to follow Onesimus' reasoning and suspicious*)   That's your problem. But if you're trying to shake me down, if you've got the notion that I'm going to

pay you off to get the ring back, you're out of your mind.
I'm not the kind that makes deals.

ONESIMUS   (*quickly*)   I'm not asking you to.

SYRISCUS   All right. I'm going to town now. When I'm
finished running some errands there, I'm coming right back
to look into what's to be done about all this. (*Exits stage
left.*)

HABROTONON   (*who has been listening in on the conversation with growing curiosity*)   Onesimus, the baby the
woman is nursing inside now, is that the one this charcoal
burner found?

ONESIMUS   So he says.

HABROTONON   Poor little baby. It's so cute.

ONESIMUS   And this ring was with it. (*Looking around
furtively and dropping his voice to a whisper*)   It's Charisius'!

HABROTONON   (*passionately, her sudden indignation
born of her resentment at her own sorry fate*)   Oh, how
could you! When there's a chance this child may actually
be your master's son, are you going to stand by and see him
brought up in slavery? I could murder you! And I'd have
every right.

ONESIMUS   (*taken aback at Habrotonon's vehemence and
on the defensive*)   But, as I was saying before, nobody
knows who the mother is.

HABROTONON   (*thoughtfully*)   Did you say he lost it
at the Festival of Artemis?

ONESIMUS   Yes, he was drunk. I heard about it from the
boy who was attending him.

HABROTONON   (*as before*)   He must have gotten in by
himself and gone after the women who were spending the
night there. The same sort of thing happened once when I
was there.

ONESIMUS   (*surprised that one of Habrotonon's profession had had an opportunity to get to a woman's festival*)
When *you* were there?

HABROTONON   Yes, last year's festival. I'd been hired to
play for a party of girls, and I joined in the fun with them.
In those days, I . . . (*Catching Onesimus' knowing and*

mocking look, she breaks off and adds sharply)   I didn't even know what a man was!

ONESIMUS   (*leering*)   Oh, sure.

HABROTONON   (*earnestly*)   I didn't, I swear it.

ONESIMUS   (*having gotten in his dig, getting back to the matter at hand*)   But this girl it happened to—do you know who she was?

HABROTONON   (*thoughtful again*)   I could find out. She was a friend of the girls I was with.

ONESIMUS   Did you happen to hear who her father was?

HABROTONON   I don't know a thing about her except that, if I saw her, I'd recognize her. She was really beautiful, I swear. And I heard she was really rich.

ONESIMUS   (*hopefully*)   Maybe it's the same one.

HABROTONON   I wouldn't know. Anyway, she was there with us, and then she wandered off somewhere. Then, all of a sudden, we see her running toward us all by herself, crying and tearing her hair. And her dress! It was one of those south Italian gowns, simply beautiful, and very sheer fabric, and it was ruined. The whole thing was just a *rag*.

ONESIMUS   (*patiently enduring the female's eternal interest in clothes and anxious to get back to the main point*)   And she had this ring?

HABROTONON   (*firmly*)   Maybe she did, but she didn't show it to me, and I'm not going to make anything up.

ONESIMUS   (*more up in the air now than even before*)   What should I do now?

HABROTONON   That's your worry. But if you've got any sense, you'll take my advice and make a clean breast of it to Charisius. If the baby belongs to a girl from a good family, why must what's happened be a secret?

ONESIMUS   First let's find out who she is. (*Pleadingly*)   Habrotonon, I need your help for this.

HABROTONON   (*quickly*)   Oh, I couldn't. Not until I know who attacked her. I'd be afraid of starting something with those girls I told you about, for no reason. You never can tell; maybe someone else, one of the men with him, got the ring as security and then lost it. When they were gambling Charisius might have thrown it into the pot, or maybe

he lost a bet and ran short and handed the ring over. When
men get to drinking, any of a thousand things like that are
bound to happen. I don't want to go looking for the girl or
breathe a word about it until I find out who attacked her.

ONESIMUS   (*nodding assent gloomily*) You've got a
point there. (*In despair*)   What is a man to do then?

HABROTONON   (*thoughtfully*)   Onesimus, listen. I've
got an idea. See if you like it. (*Pausing to make sure he is
listening and eying him closely to note the effect*)   Suppose
I pretend that the whole thing happened to me. Suppose I
take this ring and go in to see him.

ONESIMUS   (*eagerly*)   Keep talking. I'm getting the
idea.

HABROTONON   (*warming to the subject*)   The minute
he sees me with it, he'll ask me where I got it. I'll say (*melodramatically*), "At the Festival of Artemis—when I was
still a virgin." Then I'll make believe that everything that
happened to her happened to me. Most of it I know, anyway.

ONESIMUS   Terrific!

HABROTONON   And if it hits home—

ONESIMUS   (*interrupting in his excitement*)   Good,
good.

HABROTONON   —he'll fall right into the trap. He's been
drinking, you know, so he'll spill the whole story first. I
don't want to slip up anywhere, so I'll let him do the talking. I'll just say Yes to whatever he says.

ONESIMUS   Very good. God, yes. *Very* good!

HABROTONON   When I have to say something, I'll make
up the sort of thing you can't go wrong on. Like (*melodramatically*),   "Oh, you were really a brute! The way you
went after me!"

ONESIMUS   Good, good!

HABROTONON   (*as before*)   "And when you threw me
down you were so *rough!* My poor dress was absolutely
ruined!" (*Dropping the histrionics and abruptly becoming
matter-of-fact again*)   Before I do anything, I want to go
inside and get the baby. I want to cry over it, pet it—and
find out from that woman just where she got it.

ONESIMUS   (*aghast at the breakneck pace at which
things are suddenly moving*)   My god!

HABROTONON   And my last line will be (*melodramati-cally*), "Charisius! You are the father of a child!" And then I'll produce the baby.

ONESIMUS   (*maliciously*)   Habrotonon, you could make a fortune as a crook.

HABROTONON   (*deliberately ignoring him*)   If it works, and he does turn out to be the baby's father, then we'll have lots of time to look for the mother later.

ONESIMUS   (*a train of thought suddenly started in his mind by Habrotonon's last remark*)   You forgot to mention that you'll get your freedom. He'll buy it the minute he's convinced you're the mother. No doubt about it.

HABROTONON   (*deprecatorily*)   Oh, I don't know. I hope so.

ONESIMUS   So you don't know, eh? (*Coming closer to her*)   How about me, Habrotonon? Do I get any thanks for what you'll get out of all this?

HABROTONON   (*sweetly*)   Of course! You know I'll always feel that whatever I get I owe to you.

ONESIMUS   (*bluntly*)   Suppose you just don't go looking for the girl? Suppose you just double-cross me and drop the whole business? What then?

HABROTONON   (*quickly*)   My god! What makes you think I want anything to do with children? (*Fervently*) Just let me get my freedom. God knows that's all I want out of all this.

ONESIMUS   (*somewhat reassured*)   I hope you get it.

HABROTONON   Well? Do you like my idea?

ONESIMUS   I like it fine. (*Grimly*)   Because, if you play any dirty tricks, I'll let you have it. And I can do it, too. (*Relaxing his tone*)   Right now, let's see how things go.

HABROTONON   So it's a deal?

ONESIMUS   Right.

HABROTONON   (*anxious to clinch things before Onesimus has any second thoughts*)   Quick, give me the ring!

ONESIMUS   Here, take it.

HABROTONON   (*fervently, as she goes into Chaerestratus' house*)   Holy lady of Persuasion, stand by me now! Please put the right words in my mouth!

ONESIMUS   (*to himself, shaking his head in awed admir-*

ation)   The female of the species knows her way around.
When she sees she can't get her freedom through making
love, that that's a dead end, she takes another route. A poor
slob like me, with the brains knocked out of my head, I
could never figure out what to do about such things. Result
—I'll be a slave all my life. (*Brightening*)   Maybe, if she
pulls it off, I'll get something from her. I certainly deserve
it. (*Clapping a hand to his brow*)   What's the matter with
me? Lost my mind? Expect gratitude from a woman? I'll
be satisfied if she doesn't add to my troubles. Right now,
Pamphila's situation is pretty shaky. The minute Charisius
finds out it's a girl from a good family who's the mother of
his child, he's going to marry her and get rid of his wife.
Anyway, if you ask me, I've done a neat job of keeping myself in the clear; I've kept my fingers out of this mess. And,
from now on, goodbye to meddling: if anyone catches me
sticking my nose into other people's business, or talking out
of turn, I hereby give him permission to cut my tongue out.
(*Noticing someone approaching, stage left*)   But who's
this coming? (*Looking closely*)   It's Smicrines, back from
town, and he's burning up; maybe he's learned the truth
from someone. I'm going to make myself scarce. (*Hurries
into Chaerestratus' house.*)

[The second half of the act (120-odd lines) is fragmentary.
Just enough is preserved to enable us to follow the plot.
    When Smicrines comes on stage he delivers in soliloquy a
tirade that makes it clear his trip to town has only multiplied
his misgivings. This, however, is only the beginning. A cook
now comes out of Chaerestratus' house, and his lines reveal
that Habrotonon's ruse has been brilliantly successful: Charisius has ended the party, sent everybody home (this is how the
cook got into the act; he was told to pack up and go), acknowledged the baby, and installed Habrotonon in the house. By the
time the cook leaves, the old man is seething.
    And so, when Chaerestratus comes out of his house and
tries to defend Charisius, he doesn't get very far. Smicrines
vows that he's not only going to rescue his daughter from all
this, but, what's more, is going to summon Chaerestratus as
a witness and compel him to testify to the treatment she's been

subjected to. The act closes as he enters Charisius' house to get Pamphila.]

ACT IV

(*Pamphila and Smicrines emerge from Charisius' house. They have obviously been arguing. Now that Charisius has established Habrotonon in his house and plans to raise the child, Smicrines wants his daughter to have nothing more to do with him. Pamphila, loyal to her husband and desperately hopeful that some way out will be found, refuses to leave. The argument continues on stage.*)

PAMPHILA   (*stubbornly*) You've got to convince me I need to be rescued. Otherwise you'll be treating me like a slave, not a daughter.

SMICRINES   (*exasperated*) Convince you! What for? Isn't it clear as day? Pamphila, the situation cries out to high heaven. (*As she starts to move away from him*) All right. If I have to talk you into it, I'm ready. There are three things I'm going to point out to you. There's not a chance of salvaging this marriage, neither on your side, nor his. [About 28 lines are lost here, in which Smicrines evaluated the feasibility of Charisius' keeping the two women in separate households.] Think of the expense. Double each year for the women's festival in June. Double each year for the women's festival in October. He'll run through his money, you've got to realize that. And that means he's ruined, right? Now let's look at it from your side. He'll tell you he has to go out on business. He'll go out and stay out. And you'll be miserable, believe me. You'll wait around, you'll hold up dinner. And he'll be drinking with that entertainer. [Another, larger, segment of almost 100 lines is lost here in which Smicrines evaluated the feasibility of the two women living under the same roof.] A respectable girl is no match for a whore, Pamphila. She's been around, she knows all the tricks; she won't stop at anything, she knows how to get around a man.

(The rest of Smicrines' speech is lost. Apparently all his talk has no effect and, finally, he leaves. At this moment, Habrotonon comes out of Chaerestratus' house holding the baby. Her first words are addressed to someone inside.)

HABROTONON   *(through the doorway)* I'm going to take the baby out. The poor thing's been crying its heart out all this time. There's something the matter with it.

PAMPHILA   *(seeing Habrotonon, the source of her present torment, to herself)* Oh, god! Have mercy on me!

HABROTONON   *(hearing Pamphila's voice, looks up, recognizes her, and whispers to the baby, excitedly)* Baby darling, you're going to see your mommy! She came out here just at the right time!

PAMPHILA   *(to herself)* I'll get out of here.

HABROTONON   *(stationing herself near the door to Charisius' house, so Pamphila can't avoid her)* May I see you a moment, please?

PAMPHILA   *(frigidly)* Are you speaking to me?

HABROTONON   Yes. *(Pleadingly)* Please! Look at me! Do you know me? *(Aside)* She *is* the one I saw that time. *(To Pamphila, warmly)* I am *so* glad to see you!

PAMPHILA   *(confused)* But—who are you?

HABROTONON   Here, let me take your hand. Tell me, dear lady, weren't you at the Festival of Artemis last year? [A half line is lost here.]

PAMPHILA   *(suddenly noticing the necklace the baby is wearing and, disregarding the question, urgently)* Tell me, please, where did you get this child?

HABROTONON   *(quickly)* Oh, my dear, do you recognize something it's wearing? Please tell me. Don't be afraid of me!

PAMPHILA   *(still confused but sensing the glimmer of a possibility)* Aren't you the mother?

HABROTONON   *(speaking rapidly and with all the persuasion at her command)* I pretended I was—not to cheat the real mother, but to gain time to find her. And I have— just now. For you are the girl I saw that night!

PAMPHILA   *(turns away, lowers her head in shame, and*

remains silent. Then, with eyes averted and speaking in almost a whisper) Do you know who the father is?

HABROTONON (*almost shouting*) Charisius!

PAMPHILA (*straightens up, startled. Stares at Habrotonon, incredulous*) My dearest girl, are you sure of this?

HABROTONON Absolutely. (*Pointing to Charisius' house*) You *are* the mistress of this house, aren't you?

PAMPHILA Yes, yes.

HABROTONON Then thank your lucky stars. God *has* had mercy on you. (*The door of Chaerestratus' house starts to open.*) Wait! Someone's coming out next door. Take me inside your house. I'll tell you the rest of the story there.

(*The two women hurry into Charisius' house. A second later Onesimus emerges from Chaerestratus' house. It is obvious that he is considerably perturbed.*)

ONESIMUS (*to the audience*) He's going out of his mind. By god, he *is* out of his mind. He's really gone out of his mind; clean out of his mind, I swear. Charisius, I mean. Had an attack of manic depression or something. How else can you explain something like this? Just now, for the longest while he was squatting outside the back door with his ear glued to it. I guess his father-in-law must have been inside discussing the situation with Pamphila. Well, the way that man's color kept changing—I just can't talk about it. Then he bursts out with (*imitating Charisius*), "Sweetheart! What wonderful things to say!" and gives himself a blow on the head, real hard. Then, a little while later (*imitating him again*), "To think I had a wife like that! What a miserable failure I've been!" Finally, when he heard all they had to say, he went inside and there he started to rant and tear his hair and even have fits. He kept saying over and over: "I'm the guilty one. I committed that sort of act myself: I became the father of an illegitimate child. Yet I had no forgiveness in my heart, I had none to offer that poor girl who was the unlucky victim of just such an attack. I'm a brute, a pitiless brute." He keeps shouting these awful things about himself, he's all worked up, his eyes are bloodshot—I'm scared. I'm scared stiff. In his condition, if he sees me, the fellow who told on her, he's liable to kill me. That's why I sneaked out of the house. But where am I going to go? What am I going to do? I'm a goner, I'm sunk! (*The door of Chaerestratus' house opens.*) He's coming out now. God in heaven help me—if you can!

(*Having nowhere else to go, Onesimus ducks into Charisius' house. A moment later, Charisius comes out of Chaerestratus' house.*)

CHARISIUS   (*to the audience, bitterly*)   There I was act- ing like some saint, always with an eye on my reputation, reading the books on what's right and what's wrong, pure, above reproach—well, the good lord has treated me just as I deserve. He showed me up: "You, with all your wind and big talk, you poor fool, you're only human. Your wife runs into trouble through no fault of her own, and you can't take it. Well, I'm going to show the world that you've fallen as low as she. And, when she hears about it, she'll treat you with sympathy and understanding, even though at this mo- ment you're denying her everything that's her due. Every- body's going to know you for what you are—a miserable, stupid cad. The thoughts you've been having about her and what you heard her tell her father—not exactly the same, are they? She told him she had become a partner in your life and that it was her duty not to desert when trouble came along. And you, holier-than-thou Charisius, you treated her like a brute. [Six lines are lost here.] Nor will her father treat her very nicely." (*Having completed this imagi- nary divine rebuke, he paces up and down for a moment in silence. Then, defiantly*)   What do I care about her father? I'll lay it on the line to him: "Smicrines, I don't want any trouble from you. My wife's not going to leave me. What are you upsetting her for? What are you pressuring her for?"

(*At this moment Onesimus, with Habrotonon behind him, bursts out of Charisius' house. He sees Charisius and makes an abrupt about-face but it is too late; Charisius has already seen him.*)

CHARISIUS   (*eyeing him balefully*) What! You again?
ONESIMUS   (*quaking, aside*) I'm in trouble, real trouble. (*To Habrotonon*) Please! Don't desert me now!
CHARISIUS   You little sneak, were you standing here listening to what I was saying?
ONESIMUS   (*terrified*) No! I swear, I just came out.

[Thirteen lines are lost here. The altercation apparently continued until Habrotonon stepped forward to take a hand in the proceedings and presumably explained that Onesimus had given her the ring and that she had pretended the baby was hers. But this only succeeds in inciting Charisius in his overwrought state to go after Onesimus again.]

CHARISIUS   (*advancing on Onesimus menacingly*) Well, Onesimus, what have you got to say? You were testing me, eh?
ONESIMUS   (*pointing to Habrotonon*) She talked me into it, I swear to god!
CHARISIUS   (*coming still closer*) So, you little sneak, you're playing games with me, eh?
HABROTONON   (*rushing in between the two of them, frantically*) Please! Please stop this fighting! The baby's your own wedded wife's, no one else's!
CHARISIUS   (*dully*) If only it were!
HABROTONON   (*in her excitement almost shrieking*) It is, I swear it!
CHARISIUS   (*his attention finally caught by the intensity of the girl's manner*) What are you saying?
HABROTONON   The truth!
CHARISIUS   You mean it's Pamphila's baby?
HABROTONON   And yours, of course.
CHARISIUS   (*dazedly*) Pamphila's? Habrotonon, please now, don't get me all excited . . .

[About twenty lines, the last of the act, are lost here, in which Habrotonon presumably convinces him that the child is really his wife's and the three go into Charisius' house.]

ACT V

[The first eighty lines are for the most part lost. Enough is
left to show that Chaerestratus and a friend—or, more likely,
a servant—named Simias, are involved and that the topic of
their discussion is Habrotonon; very likely the audience
learned that she had gotten the freedom she yearned for so
passionately. They leave and the stage is empty. A second
later Smicrines enters, stage left, dragging after him Sophrona, Pamphila's old nurse, the one who had helped her dis-
pose of the child at the outset. Smicrines, in complete ignorance of all that has happened, is bent on rescuing his daughter
—and what's left of the dowry.]

SMICRINES   Sophrona, so help me, I'll bash in that skull
of yours. Are you telling me what to do? So, "It's very
rash of me to carry off my daughter," is it, you lying old
hag? I suppose I should sit back and waste my breath talking about the dowry I turned over, while that fine husband
of hers swallows it up? You're telling me to do that too, eh?
Don't you know it's better to strike while the iron is hot?
(*As she opens her mouth to answer*)   Another word out
of you and you'll be sorry! (*To himself*)   What am I—a
defendant before Sophrona? (*To her again*)   *You* go and
reason with her—if ever you get to see her. Because, Sophrona, so help me, when we go home from here—remember
that pond we passed?—I'm going to drown you there if I
have to hold you under water all night. I'm going to make
you see things my way and put an end to this taking sides
against me. (*Reaches the door of Charisius' house and tries
to open it.*)   This door is locked; I've got to bang on it.
(*Shouting*)   Inside there, somebody open this door! Open
up, I say! (*Moves off to the side, pulling Sophrona after
him, to see if any servants are around.*)

(*Onesimus comes to the door. Now that everything has
ended so happily, he has been restored to favor, and has re-
sumed his former role of the worldly wise sophisticate.*)

ONESIMUS   (*to himself as he opens the door*)   Who's knocking at this door, anyway? Oh, it's that grouch Smicrines, coming for his dowry and his daughter.

SMICRINES   (*snarling*)   Yes! It's Smicrines, damn you, and with good reason! A sensible businessman doesn't waste time. The way you people are robbing me—it's unbelievable! In the name of god—

ONESIMUS   (*interrupting with a calculatedly irritating patience, like a kindly priest dealing with a not overly bright member of his congregation*)   Now, Smicrines, do you think god has so much time on his hands that he can go around parceling out a daily dose of good and bad to each one of us?

SMICRINES   (*testily*)   What are you talking about?

ONESIMUS   (*as before*)   I'll explain it to you. At a rough guess there are a thousand cities in the world. Say, thirty thousand people in each. Now, can god go around damning or saving every single one of them? How? Some working day you'd have him put in! What then? Are you going to say that he doesn't care about us mortals? Not at all—he's given each of us our character to be the captain of our soul. This is the guardian that's always with us; it damns us when we treat it badly and saves us when we don't. This is our god, and this is what's responsible for whether we live happily or unhappily, every one of us. Just win its favor by not doing anything stupid or out of place, and you'll live happily.

SMICRINES   (*snarling*)   And I suppose, you little sneak, my character is doing something stupid right now?

ONESIMUS   (*solemnly*)   It's ruining you.

SMICRINES   (*outraged*)   Of all the insolence!

ONESIMUS   (*with an air of great patience and righteousness*)   Smicrines, do you think it's the right thing for a man to do, to take a daughter away from her husband?

SMICRINES   Who's talking about the right thing? It's simply something that's got to be done.

ONESIMUS   (*to Sophrona, shaking his head*)   You see? According to this fellow's way of thinking, a man must do the wrong thing. (*Shaking his head commiseratingly*) Some other god, not his character, is ruining this man. (*To Smicrines*)   Well, this time just as you were rushing to do

something wicked, sheer luck has saved you. You've arrived
just in time to find everybody reconciled and all your troubles solved. (*Sternly*) But, Smicrines, I warn you—don't
let me catch you doing anything rash again. (*Grandly*)
Right now I consider you absolved of any such charges. You
may go in and say hello to your grandson.

SMICRINES   (*fuming*)   Grandson? I'll have you horse-
whipped!

ONESIMUS   (*scornfully*)   You thought you were so
smart. You were as thick as the others! Is that the way you
kept an eye on a grown-up daughter? Look at the result—
now we have a prodigy to raise, a baby that needed only five
months of pregnancy!

SMICRINES   (*utterly confused*)   I don't know what
you're talking about.

ONESIMUS   I'll bet the old woman here does. (*Turning
to Sophrona*) Sophrona, my master was the one who grabbed
and dragged her off from the dancing at the Festival of
Artemis—understand me?

SOPHRONA   (*nodding vigorously*)   Oh, yes.

ONESIMUS   And now they've recognized each other and
everything is fine.

SMICRINES   (*to Sophrona*)   What does he mean, you
lying old hag?

SOPHRONA   (*quoting from Euripides' play, the* Auge, *in
which Heracles identified a child of his by a ring*)

> For Nature wished it so. She spurns all laws—
> And fashioned womankind for just this cause.

SMICRINES   (*more confused than ever*)   Have you gone
out of your mind?

SOPHRONA   (*sharply*)   I'll recite a whole speech from
the *Auge* if you don't start using your brains, Smicrines.

SMICRINES   (*testily*)   You and your histrionics are going to make me lose my temper. You really understand what
he's talking about?

SOPHRONA   (*firmly*)   Every word.

ONESIMUS   Believe me, she knew about it a long time ago.

SMICRINES   This is terrible!

SOPHRONA   It's the best thing that's ever happened! (*To Onesimus*)   If what you say is true and the baby . . .

[The rest of the act is lost. but the plot is virtually complete at this point: Charisius and Pamphila had been reconciled by the end of Act IV, and now Smicrines joins them. If Habrotonon and Onesimus had not received their freedom earlier, they very likely were given it before the final curtain.]

She Who Was Shorn

DRAMATIS PERSONAE

POLEMON, a wealthy, young professional army officer
SOSIAS, his orderly (slave)
GLYCERA, a free-born, but poor, girl living with Polemon
DORIS, her maid (slave)
MOSCHION, a young man about town, adopted son of
  Myrrhina
DAVUS, servant (slave) of Moschion's family
PATAECUS, an elderly friend of Polemon
[MYRRHINA, foster-mother of Moschion]

SCENE

A street in Corinth. Three house entrances front on it: on one side is that of Myrrhina and Moschion, her adopted son; in the middle is that of Polemon; on the other side that of Pataecus. The exit on stage left leads downtown, that on stage right to the open country.

ACT I

[About 120 lines are lost before the preserved portion begins, but we can deduce with a fair degree of certainty what they told.

The first scene introduced the protagonists of the play, Polemon and Glycera. Polemon was a young but experienced professional army officer who had spent all his adult years in the field and always among men; though basically of a good, even fine, character, he could at times act violently and impulsively, a failing that had hardly been helped by his way of life. He had been successful in his chosen career and had made enough money to buy a house and settle down. He had even been lucky enough to come upon a very desirable girl to live with. Glycera was young, attractive, and charming, but, since she was poor—in other words, had no dowry—life as Polemon's common-law wife offered her, despite its obvious disadvantages, as comfortable a mode of existence as she could ever have hoped for. Moreover, she at the very least admired and respected him, and perhaps even loved him, while he was unquestionably very much in love with her.

After presenting the two, the scene must then have revealed the event that gives the play its name. Polemon, who had been away on campaign, returned unexpectedly one evening; the first sight that met his eyes was Glycera embracing Moschion, his neighbor's son, a pampered young playboy who rather fancied himself a ladies' man. Polemon, reacting instinctively, inflicted on Glycera an injury more visible and humiliating and lasting than the most merciless beating would have been. He treated her as the French did the girls who had taken German lovers during World War II: he cut off her hair. A moment later, as so often happens after an unthinking act, he was appalled by what he had done; unable to bear the sight, he fled into the house of his neighbor and friend, Pataecus.

The stage is now empty and a formal Prologue enters, Lady Ignorance, to tell the audience some facts it needs to know in order to follow the plot; she is a fitting enough choice for Prologue since ignorance is, in a sense, the mainspring for the play's action. Her words make clear both why Glycera was so poor and why she had been in the embrace of the boy next door.

The story she tells is this. Eighteen years ago, an old woman found in the fields an infant set of twins, a boy and a girl, and took them home. From this point on, we have the Prologue's own words.]

LADY IGNORANCE   She kept the girl but gave the boy to
a rich woman—(*gesturing toward the house alongside
Polemon's*) she lives here—who had no children of her own.
That's the way it happened.

Well, the years passed and, what with the war and things
at Corinth going from bad to worse, the old woman was at
the end of her rope. The girl was now grown up—she's the
one you saw in the first scene—and, when that young hot-
head you've just seen came along, since he was no stranger
but a local Corinthian boy and had fallen in love with the
girl, the old woman gave her to him, letting him think it was
her own daughter. But because she was by this time quite
old and weary, and had a feeling that her end was at hand,
she decided not to keep anything secret from the girl. The
old woman told her she was a foundling, gave her the baby
clothes she had been found in, and disclosed to her the unexpected news that she had a blood brother. The old woman
did this because she was minded of the troubles that always
happen in life, occasions when the girl would need some
help, and, so far as she could see, the boy was her only relative. Besides, she wanted to guard against the possibility
that through ignorance, through my doing, the two might
involuntarily get involved with each other; for the old
woman was well aware that the boy was rich and drank too
much and the girl attractive and young, and that there was
nothing secure about the union she had entered into.

Now, the old woman died and, not long ago, the officer
bought this house (*gesturing toward Polemon's house*). Although the girl has been living next door, she's kept quiet
about having a brother. She doesn't want to disturb things
when his prospects look so bright. She wants him to enjoy
everything his good fortune has brought him. Well, as luck
would have it, last night he saw her when she happened to
send her maid out on an errand: as I mentioned, he's the type
that will make advances and when he went walking he always saw to it that he stayed near her house. He saw her
at the door, ran right up, took her in his arms, and kissed
her. She knew it was her brother, of course, and didn't try
to break away—and at that moment along comes the officer
and sees everything. You've heard what happened next from

his own lips: how he took himself off telling her that he wanted to see her later and how she stood there crying, brokenhearted, over the way circumstances wouldn't permit her to do what she wanted.

Now, all this has erupted because of what's to come: to get him (*with a gesture toward Polemon's house*) to whip himself into a lather—it's all my doing, of course; it's not his way to be like that—, to get the disclosures that are in store under way, and to have the twins find out who they are. If any of you are revolted by what's happened and consider it disgraceful, you'll change your mind. God can turn even evil into good. Goodbye, dear audience, be kind to us, and enjoy what you are going to see.

(*It is the morning after Polemon's violent act. The door of Pataecus' house, where Polemon is now staying, opens and Sosias, his orderly, comes out. Sosias is a tough old-line army man, and he takes a very dim view of such unmilitary conduct as getting upset over a woman.*)

SOSIAS   (*to himself, scornfully*) Well, our man who's so set against women having hair, who was stomping around a while ago spoiling for a fight, is now flat on his back crying his eyes out. Just now, when I left, breakfast was being served and all his friends had rallied around to buck him up. (*Gesturing toward Polemon's house, where Glycera was still staying*) Since he's got no way of knowing what's going on here, he's purposely sent me out to get him a coat. (*Grumbling*) He doesn't really need it. What's he want to do, give me some exercise?

(*At this moment the door of Polemon's house opens and Doris, Glycera's maid, comes out. She turns and speaks to Glycera inside.*)

DORIS   (*through the doorway*) I'll go and see, ma'am.
SOSIAS   (*to himself*) It's Doris. (*Admiringly, since he has not seen her since he and Polemon had left to take the field*) Look at her—not bad! Nothing wrong with the way these girls are living, so far as I can see. But I'd better get

going. (*As Doris leaves the door of Polemon's house, Sosia
enters it.*)

DORIS   (*to herself as she crosses to Myrrhina's house*)
There's nobody around outside; I'll have to knock. (*Indignantly*) I pity the poor girl who has an army man for a
husband. They're all a bunch of lawbreakers; you can't trust
any of them. What my poor mistress has to put up with!
(*Shouting*) Hey, someone open the door!

(*Someone finally does open up, and Doris enters Myrrhina's
house. A second later Sosias emerges from Polemon's house
with a coat over his arm—despite Sosias' grumbling, Polemon
could well use the coat since he had fled to Pataecus' house
with nothing but the clothes on his back. Sosias walks to
Pataecus' door and knocks.*)

SOSIAS   (*to himself*)   He'll be delighted to learn now
that she's crying. That's just what he's after. (*As a servant
answers his knock*) Please tell . . .

[About seventy lines are missing here, but what happened
can be reconstructed. Sosias disappeared into Pataecus' house
with the coat. Doris and Myrrhina then came on stage. Doris
explained the situation to Myrrhina and asked her to take
Glycera in. She agreed, Glycera hurried over, and Myrrhina
sent the family servant, Davus, with a group of slaves to trans-
fer Glycera's possessions. Davus responded with alacrity—he
was under the impression that Myrrhina was aiding and abet-
ting a love affair for that pampered son of hers. When the
text resumes, he and his men have left Polemon's house and
are approaching Myrrhina's door.]

DAVUS   (*hustling his squad, loaded down with Glycera's
belongings, into Myrrhina's house*)   Boys, there's a mob
of youngster's heading this way, and they're drunk. (*To
himself*) My congratulations to our mistress—she's moving
the girl into our house. That's what I call a mother! I've
got to find Moschion. If you ask me, this is just the time for
him to get here—and fast!

(*Davus goes off, stage left. The stage is now empty, and a chorus—the "mob of youngsters" Davus had mentioned— enters and dances an entr'acte.*)

ACT II

(*Davus and Moschion enter, stage left. Moschion is a dashing, handsome young fellow, fastidiously groomed, and wearing clothes that, although obviously expensive, are a trifle too flashy to be in the best of taste. More than his dress, however, his whole bearing reveals at a glance the spoiled, only son of an indulgent mother.*)

MOSCHION   (*menacingly*)   Davus, you're a godforsaken faker. You've told me lots of things before that turned out to be lies. If you're lying to me now—

DAVUS   If I'm lying to you now, you can hang me this minute.

MOSCHION   That's letting you off too easy.

DAVUS   (*unabashed*)   Then treat me like your worst enemy. But supposing it's true? Suppose you really find the girl in your house? Since I arranged the whole deal for you —I had to talk for hours to get the girl to move in, and to get your mother to take her in and do everything you'd want —what do I get out of it?

MOSCHION   (*blandly*)   Well, Davus, what would you like best to do for a living?

DAVUS   (*warily*)   Let me think it over.

MOSCHION   (*who, obviously having taken a lot from Davus in the past, is glad to get the chance to turn the tables for once*)   Don't you think making little ones out of big ones would suit you perfectly?

DAVUS   (*in alarm, not sure whether Moschion is joking*)   The rock pile? Me?

MOSCHION   (*to the audience, pointing to Davus*)   If you ask me, he's heading right in that direction.

DAVUS   (*with a shudder*)   Don't mention the word!

MOSCHION   (*assuming an air of serious deliberation*)

I'd like to see you become military governor of Greece and
paymaster general of the armies.

DAVUS   What? And have a gang of soldiers slit my throat
when they catch my fingers in the till?

MOSCHION   Why don't you become commissioner of public works? Then you could really steal. You could pocket
eighty-five per cent of every contract and nobody'd notice it.

DAVUS   (*very seriously*)   Moschion, I'd like to run a little
stall downtown, sell groceries or cheese. I swear, I don't
want to become a millionaire. No, that's what I'd really like.

MOSCHION   (*putting on an air of being incensed at him
for not having a more ambitious spirit*)   What? Like some
old hag of a peddler?

DAVUS   I just want my three squares a day. And I say
I've earned it. I told you what I did for you.

MOSCHION   All right. Go peddle cheeses, and god be with
you.

DAVUS   Amen to that, as they say. (*As they reach the
door of Myrrhina's house*) Well, the girl you're dying for is
here. So, in you go.

MOSCHION   Good idea; that's what I'll do. And now it's
up to me to hand her a line and get the laugh on a certain
damned goldbraided colonel.

DAVUS   Right.

MOSCHION   But, first, Davus, you go in and scout the
whole situation. Find out what she's doing, where my
mother is, how they feel about my coming in. I don't need
to go into details with you in this sort of thing; you're a
smart boy.

DAVUS   I'm off.

MOSCHION   (*calling out as Davus goes into the house*)
I'll walk around in front of the door here and wait for you.
(*To himself, as he struts up and down*) She let me know
how the land lay when I went up to her yesterday evening.
When I ran toward her, she didn't run away; just put her
arms around me and kissed me (*Smugly*) You ask me, I
think I'm not so bad to look at, and not so bad to be with,
by god. I'm the type girls go for. But knock on wood and
fingers crossed!

(*Davus comes running out.*)

DAVUS (*excitedly*) Moschion, she's got herself all dressed up, and she's sitting down inside!

MOSCHION (*to himself, rapturously*) Swetheart!

DAVUS Your mother's walking around arranging god knows what. But breakfast is on the table and I think, from what's going on, they're waiting for you.

MOSCHION (*smugly, to the audience*) Didn't I tell you? I'm not bad, not bad at all. (*To Davus*) Did you tell them I was here?

DAVUS No, I didn't.

MOSCHION Then you go right inside and tell them!

DAVUS Right. Back I go. (*Hurries back into the house.*)

MOSCHION (*to himself*) She's going to be embarrassed when I come in, of course, and she'll hide her face. They all do it. The first step is to kiss my mother and win her over completely; get the flattery going and spend every minute just doing things for her. You'd think this was all her affair, the way she's handled it! Ah, someone's coming out. (*Davus comes out and walks slowly toward Moschion, shaking his head; obviously he is puzzled about something.*) Hey, what is this? Davus! What are you hanging back like that for?

DAVUS God in heaven! The whole thing's crazy. I went in and I told your mother you were here and she says: "None of that! How did he hear about it? Did you go and tell him this poor girl was so frightened she had to come running to us?" "Sure," says I. "Oh, I hope you drop dead!" says she, "And you can just clear out of here right now. I'm busy." What more can I tell you? We've lost everything. She certainly wasn't overjoyed to hear you were around.

MOSCHION (*eyeing him balefully*) I'm going to give it to you—you pulled a fast one on me!

DAVUS Don't be ridiculous. Your mother—

MOSCHION (*suddenly aware of the implications of the conversation just reported to him*) What did you just say? Something about her not coming here of her own free will? She didn't come because of me? (*Accusingly*) Then just how did you talk her into coming here for my sake?

DAVUS   (*with an air of utter incredulity*)   I said I talked
her into coming? As god's my witness I did nothing of the
sort! (*With injured innocence*) You couldn't have said anything more untrue.

MOSCHION   (*taking a threatening step toward him*)
You didn't tell me just now that you talked my mother into
taking her in for my sake?

DAVUS   Well, you see—(*as Moschion raises an arm*) yes,
I did say that. Yes, it comes back to me now.

MOSCHION   And that you thought she was doing it just
for me?

DAVUS   I don't want to say that—(*as Moschion's arm goes
up again*) but I admit I urged her.

MOSCHION   (*with an air of finality*)   That does it. Come
here!

DAVUS   (*still acting the innocent*)   Where?

MOSCHION   (*grimly*)   Not very far.

DAVUS   (*sparring desperately for time*)   Moschion,
there's something or other you ought to know—er—I—er—
at that time—er—(*as Moschion takes a threatening step
closer*) wait, just a second!

MOSCHION   (*between his teeth*)   You're playing games
with me!

DAVUS   No, I swear to god! (*Suddenly getting an idea to
get himself out of this fix*) Listen to me, please. Maybe she
doesn't want to give in, you understand, right off the bat,
just like that. Maybe she feels she ought to get to know
you and hear what you've got to say. Sure, that's it. Remember, this is no chorus girl or cheap whore who's come to you.

MOSCHION   Now you're making sense again.

DAVUS   Give it a try. You know how it is. She's left her
house—was I playing games about that? So if you'll just be
willing to hold off for three or four days, she'll come around.
I've got it on good authority. (*Desperately*) You have to
listen to me now!

MOSCHION   (*with ominous calm*)   You've figured out a
fine full four-day furlough for me. All right, Davus, I'll just
tie you up in the meantime. Where do you want to be left?
(*Dropping his assumed calm, angrily*) A minute ago you
were making sense and now you're back to nonsense.

DAVUS   Give me a chance to think in peace, will you? Why don't you reform and be a nice fellow—and go inside.

MOSCHION   (*suspiciously*)   And let you run away?

DAVUS   (*scornfully*)   Oh, sure. How far do you think I'd get, anyway, on the money I've got? No, I've got an idea that if you go inside you could straighten things out a bit.

MOSCHION   All right. I agree. You win. (*He goes into the house.*)

DAVUS   (*mopping his brow, to himself*)   Lord, that was close! I'm still shivering. This isn't going to be as easy as I thought.

(*Davus is just about to follow Moschion into Myrrhina's house when he notices Sosias come out of Pataecus' house. Sosias had earlier brought Polemon a coat to wear; now he is bringing back part of Polemon's uniform. He is getting fed up with these comings and goings and is grumbling as he comes on stage.*)

SOSIAS   (*to himself*)   He's sent me back with this tunic and sword to get a look at what she's doing and report back to him. I'm just about ready to tell him I caught her lover in the house—*that*'d bring him here on the double. No, I won't; I pity him too much. Never saw such a poor devil, not even in a nightmare. What a homecoming he's had! (*Enters Polemon's house.*)

DAVUS   (*to himself, unobserved by Sosias*)   So, the army's back, eh? That's not so good; no, sir, not good at all. (*Suddenly aware of what would happen if Myrrhina's husband were to barge in and discover what was going on*) But I haven't yet entered the chief debit in the books: if my master happens to get back from the country in a hurry and makes an appearance—what a riot *he'll* raise!

(*The door of Polemon's house opens and Sosias appears. He has found out that Glycera is gone. As he comes out, he shouts at the servants inside.*)

SOSIAS   (*through the doorway*)   You let her get away, you godforsaken dumbbells; you let her get out of the house!

DAVUS   (*to himself*)   Here he comes back—and he's
sore! I'd better get out of the way. (*Moves off to a spot on
the side from where, unobserved, he can overhear and keep
an eye on Sosias.*)

(*Sosias starts toward Pataecus' house to make his report,
and then suddenly stops short as a thought strikes him.*)

SOSIAS   (*to himself*)   That's it! She's told us to go to the
devil, and she's gone off to her lover next door.
DAVUS   (*to himself*)   That's no orderly, that's a mind
reader our colonel has there. He's hit the nail on the head.
SOSIAS   (*turning around and going up to Myrrhina's
house*)   I'll knock on the door. (*He knocks.*)

(*Davus, deciding the time is ripe to take a hand, comes out
of his hiding place.*)

DAVUS   Hey, you! What the devil are you after? Where
do you think you're going?
SOSIAS   (*gesturing toward Myrrhina's house*)   You belong here?
DAVUS   Maybe. But what are you poking your nose
around here for?

(*At this point, in answer to Sosias' knock, Doris comes to
the door. Sensing what is happening, she moves off to the side
to listen.*)

SOSIAS   (*angrily*)   God in heaven, are you people out of
your mind? Some nerve you have to keep a free-born woman
locked up in violation of the rights of her legal guardian!
DORIS   (*aside*)   Just like a sniveling good-for-nothing
like you to think up something like that.
SOSIAS   (*with a sweeping gesture toward Polemon's
house*)   Maybe you think we don't have guts? We're not
men, eh?
DAVUS   (*sneering*)   Men? Tin soldiers!
SOSIAS   (*backing down a bit since all he could muster was

a parcel of slaves and since his own courage had a way of getting unstuck easily)   Yeah? But when an iron man leads them, we won't have any trouble taking you people on.

DAVUS   This is a damned outrage!

SOSIAS   Come on, admit you've got her. (*Turning to Polemon's house and calling to one of the servants there*) Hey, you, Hilarion! Come here! (*No movement from the house. He turns back to Davus.*)   He's gone somewhere. He happened to see it all, and he says you've got her.

DAVUS   We don't have her.

SOSIAS   You people are going to feel sorry for this. Who do you think you're fooling around with, anyway? What sort of nonsense is this? Why, we'll launch a full-scale attack, storm that miserable shack of yours, and take it in a minute. Better tell lover-boy to strip for action.

DAVUS   (*shaking his head in mock sorrow*)   You poor guy—pretty tough waiting around all this time because you thought we had her in our house.

SOSIAS   Our commando troops will sweep the field before you can bat an eye—tin soldiers, eh?

DAVUS   (*scornfully*)   I was joking: you're just a hick.

SOSIAS   (*blustering*)   Well, you city types—

DAVUS   (*who knows that Sosias is just so much wind, and has listened to enough of it, interrupting*)   Listen—we haven't got her.

SOSIAS   (*screaming with rage*)   Yahhh! Wait till I get my spear—

DAVUS   (*turning away, disgustedly*)   Oh, go to hell. I'm going in now—and I'm staying there until you come to your senses.

(*Davus goes into Myrrhina's house. As Sosias stands there, baffled, Doris calls to him from the spot where she has been standing unobserved.*)

DORIS   Sosias!

SOSIAS   (*swiveling around and starting to bluster the minute he sees her*)   Doris, just come over here, and I'll give it to you. You're to blame for all this.

DORIS   (*urgently*) Oh, Sosias, please! Please tell him
that she got terribly frightened and ran away to some
woman.

SOSIAS   (*puzzled*)   To some woman? Got terribly frightened?

DORIS   That's right. She's gone to Myrrhina, her neighbor
here. So help me, it's the truth!

SOSIAS   (*disgusted and infuriated*)   Don't you realize
where she's gone? That's just where her lover is! (*He takes
a step toward her.*)

[About sixty lines are lost at this point. Presumably Sosias
reported what he had found out to Polemon and suggested
they follow out the threat he had made to Davus and break
into Myrrhina's house. To Sosias this procedure had two ad-
vantages: it would enable him to get even with Davus, and
Polemon to carry Glycera off by force. Since Polemon was by
training prejudiced in favor of such pseudo-military actions
in the first place, and since he had had too much to drink in
the second, he agreed. They sallied forth at the head of a mot-
ley group of household slaves; even Habrotonon, a courtesan
who had been hired to help cheer Polemon up, joined the
"army." Fortunately Pataecus, the only clear head around,
got them to agree to hold off until he had a chance to talk with
Myrrhina and find out whatever he could that would throw
light on Glycera's reasons for choosing to flee there.]

ACT III

(*As the act opens, Polemon and Sosias and their ragtail
army are milling about in front of Myrrhina's house. The door
opens and Pataecus, his parley with Myrrhina finished, comes
out.*

*Pataecus is old enough to be Glycera's father. You can see
at a glance why Polemon had gone to him for help: his face
is that of a man who has endured a good deal of suffering
and from it learned compassion and calmness and resignation;
clearly he is someone you can come to for sympathy and understanding, and can trust implicitly.*

Sosias, with Polemon at his side and a few men at his back and more than a few drinks inside, is in no mood to give up the present promising opportunity to square accounts with Davus. The moment he catches sight of Pataecus he calls out to Polemon.)

SOSIAS   (*excitedly*)   Here he comes—and they've bribed him. Believe me, he's out to betray you and your army.

PATAECUS   (*to Sosias, firmly but not unkindly*)   Now, stop playing soldier boy and be a good fellow and go on home and sleep it off. You're not in good shape. (*Turning to Polemon*) I'll talk to you: you're not so drunk.

POLEMON   (*pained*)   Not so drunk? All I've had is just about one drink, damn it! I could see all this coming, so I kept an eye on myself.

PATAECUS   Good. (*Firmly*)   Now, I want you to do what I tell you.

POLEMON   (*quietly*)   What do you want me to do?

PATAECUS   (*relieved at this reaction*)   Now you're talking the way you should. All right, I'll tell you what it is.

SOSIAS   (*realizing that Pataecus is on the point of winning out, shouts to Habrotonon, who has brought her flute with her and is acting as bugler for this "army"*)   Habrotonon! Sound the charge!

PATAECUS   (*to Polemon, mildly exasperated*)   First, will you please send him away with that army of his?

SOSIAS   (*to Pataecus, shouting*)   What a way to fight a war! Demobilize the army? What we need is a full-scale attack! (*To Polemon*) This here Pataecus is ruining everything I've done. What's he know about being an officer?

POLEMON   (*losing his temper, to Sosias*)   For god's sake, get out of here!

SOSIAS   (*grumbling*)   All right, all right, I'm going. (*As he lurches away, he passes near the tempting figure of Habrotonon.*) Habrotonon, I really thought there was a job for you here. If a fellow wants to make an attack (*leering at her*) you're handy to have around; you know how to take a position. (*She eludes him as he makes a pass at her.*) What are you running away for, you whore? Embarrassed—you? This bothers you? (*Sosias, followed by his "army" moves off*

*to the side of the stage, leaving Polemon and Pataecus alone
in the center.*)

PATAECUS   Now, Polemon, if something like what you've
told me about had happened and the woman were your
wife—

POLEMON   (*interrupting impatiently*)   What a thing to
say, Pataecus! She *is*.

PATAECUS   Ah, there's a difference.

POLEMON   (*raising his voice in his vehemence*)   I've always thought of her as my wife.

PATAECUS   You don't have to shout. (*Gently*) All right,
who betrothed her to you?

POLEMON   (*taken aback by the question*)   Who betrothed her to me? (*Weakly*) She did.

PATAECUS   Very good. Maybe at one time she did like
you. But she doesn't any longer. And, since you've treated
her in a way you shouldn't have, she's left you.

POLEMON   (*aggrieved*)   What are you saying? In a way
I shouldn't have? Now that's the most unkind cut of all!

PATAECUS   I'm sure you'll admit that what you're doing
now is madness. (*Vehemently*) What are you after? Who's
this person you're out to abduct anyway? That girl is her
own mistress. (*Firmly*) When a lover's not doing well, he
has only one course left—persuasion.

POLEMON   (*indignantly*)   What about the fellow who
ruined her while I was away? Hasn't he done me a wrong?

PATAECUS   (*sympathetically but firmly*)   He certainly
has—and if you ever have it out with him, you can take him
to court. But if you try any rough stuff, he'll have the law
on you and he'll win. What he did gives you a legal cause of
action, not carte blanche to go after your own revenge.

POLEMON   (*in desperation*)   Not even now? (*that is,
after, as he supposes, Glycera has been seduced into leaving*)

PATAECUS   Not even now.

POLEMON   (*wildly*)   God in heaven, I don't know what
to say—except that I'll burst a blood vessel! Glycera's left
me. Pataecus, you hear? She's left me! Glycera! (*Getting
control of himself with a visible effort*) Well, you're a good
friend of hers and you've often chatted with her in the

past, so, if you think it's the right thing to do, please go and
have a talk with her. I beg you, be my intermediary.

PATAECUS   As you see, I do think it's the right thing.

POLEMON   (*anxiously*)   You're a good talker of course,
aren't you, Pataecus?

PATAECUS   (*dryly*)   Pretty good.

POLEMON   (*his control slipping away, and starting to
talk wildly again*)   You've got to be good, Pataecus. It's
the only way to save the situation. If I've ever done her the
least wrong—if I don't spend every minute trying—if you'd
only take a look at the clothes I've bought her— (*Starts
to pull him into his house.*)

PATAECUS   (*anxious to get going on his difficult mission,
and holding back*)   Thank you, but—

POLEMON   (*brushing aside Pataecus' reluctance and pulling him toward the door*)   In the name of god, Pataecus,
come look at them! Then you'll really feel sorry for me.

PATAECUS   (*to himself, exasperated at the delay*)   Oh,
for god's sake!

POLEMON   Come on. What dresses! And you ought to see
how she looks when she puts one of them on. You've probably never seen her.

PATAECUS   (*in a forlorn effort to get out of going inside*)   Yes, I have.

POLEMON   (*absorbed in his own thoughts and not hearing him*)   With that tall figure of hers, she sure was an
eyeful. (*Getting hold of himself again*)   But what am I doing
babbling about tall figures and things that don't concern us
now? I must be out of my mind.

PATAECUS   (*soothingly*)   No, no; not at all.

POLEMON   You mean that? Oh, but you've got to take a
look at those clothes. Come on in. (*Literally hauling the re-
luctant Pataecus into the house*)   After you.

PATAECUS   (*resignedly*)   I'm coming.

(*The two enter Polemon's house, followed by the "army"
and, in the rear, Sosias. He is just lurching through the door
when Moschion comes out of Myrrhina's house.*)

MOSCHION   (*to the retreating army*)   All right. Inside
with the whole damn bunch of you. On the double. (*To himself, quoting a line of poetry*) "With lance in hand at me
they sprang." They couldn't storm a bird's nest, not a
filthy gang like that. (*Imitating Davus' way of speaking*)
"They've got a real regiment," he tells me. It's a great regiment, all right. Look at it. (*Pointing to Sosias reeling
through the doorway*) One man. (*He paces up and down,
deeply troubled; to the audience*) There are a lot of fellows
in a bad way these days—with one thing and another,
there's a bumper crop of them right now all over Greece—
but I don't think there's a man among them all as badly off
as I am. As soon as I went in, I didn't do any of the things
I usually do—didn't go in to see my mother, didn't ring for
any of the servants—I just went into a back room out of
everybody's way and I lay down. I was all set. I sent Davus
to my mother to tell her that I was home—just that, nothing
else. Well, he finds their breakfast still on the table, forgets
all about me, and stays to stow away a meal. In the meantime, I was lying there thinking to myself, "Any minute
my mother will be here with a message from my sweetheart
telling me under what arrangement she says she'll come to
me." I was working up a little speech myself—

[About 157 lines are lost at this point. Somehow or other,
during this portion of the play, Moschion learned some highly
disquieting news: that Davus had duped him and Glycera had
come to his house not to join him but to escape from Polemon;
and that he is a foundling. He was even shown some of the
objects—"birth tokens"—that had been found with him.
    Toward the end of this missing section, Pataecus and Gly-
cera came on stage. Pataecus presumably pleaded Polemon's
cause as he had promised and offered her generous terms if
she would come back. When the text resumes, Glycera is presenting her side of the matter, indignantly making clear to him
the reason for her move next door. We are by now somewhere
in Act IV.]

ACT IV

(Glycera and Pataecus are standing in front of Myrrhina's house. She is refuting Pataecus' suspicion—which he had got from Polemon—that she had fled to Myrrhina's to join Moschion as a mistress.)

GLYCERA   *(vehemently)*   My dear man, if that were the case, how could I possibly have run to his mother? Obviously I didn't come here to be his wife; *(bitterly and with irony that is, of course, lost on Pataecus)* our different family backgrounds, you know. Well, if not that, then did I come to be his mistress? In that case, for god's sake wouldn't I have done everything I could to keep it a secret from his parents—and wouldn't he have too? But he went right ahead and introduced me to his father [*she is referring to Myrrhina's husband*]. Would I have deliberately acted so senselessly? Deliberately made an enemy of Myrrhina, and left all of you with an impression of me that you could never get rid of? *(Her bitterness now mingled with anguish)* Have I no sense of shame, Pataecus? Did you come here because you were convinced, like the others, by what you had heard? Did you take me for that sort of girl?

PATAECUS   *(with conviction)*   God forbid! And may heaven help you convince everybody else that what you tell me is true. As for myself, I'm convinced.

GLYCERA   But I still want you to go away. *(Bitterly)* Let him insult some other girl from now on.

PATAECUS   *(soothingly)*   It was a terrible thing to do, but he didn't really mean it.

GLYCERA   *(as before)*   It was an ungodly thing to do. My god, you wouldn't even treat a slave girl that way!

[Sixteen lines are lost here in which Glycera presumably revealed to Patacaeus that she was a girl of good family and asserted that she had birth tokens to prove it. When the text resumes, she is talking about them. As it happens, the chest they were in was still in Polemon's house; she had left it there in her distraught state and, since it had been hidden away, Davus and his squad had overlooked it when they transferred her belongings.]

GLYCERA   I got these birth tokens from my mother and father and I've made a practice of always having them at my side where I can keep an eye on them.

PATAECUS   Well, what do you want?

GLYCERA   I want them brought here (*pointing to Myrrhina's house*).

PATAECUS   Then you're going to give Polemon up once and for all? (*She nods resolutely. He sighs resignedly.*) All right, my dear; now, what do you want from me?

GLYCERA   I want your permission to take them.

PATAECUS   All right—although I think it's ridiculous. (*Returning to the attack*) You ought to look at all sides—

GLYCERA   (*cutting him short*)   I know what's best for me.

PATAECUS   Well, if that's the way you feel . . . Do any of the servants know where these things of yours are?

GLYCERA   Doris does.

PATAECUS   Have someone call her out here. (*Pataecus is hard to discourage. As a servant goes off to fetch Doris, he makes one last try*) Glycera, for god's sake, while there's still a chance, on the terms I've been telling you about—

(*At this point Doris, answering the summons, comes out of Myrrhina's house. Doris is in tears—her emotions are easily engaged and the whole affair has been getting her down.*)

DORIS   Ma'am!

GLYCERA   What's the matter?

DORIS   All this trouble!

GLYCERA   Doris, bring out that chest, you know, the one with those embroidered things in it that I gave you to take care of. Come on! What are you crying about? (*Doris goes off into Polemon's house.*)

PATAECUS   God in heaven, I've put up with . . .

[About 8 lines are lost here. When the text resumes, Doris

has brought out the chest and Glycera and Pataecus are discussing a piece of fabric with embroidered figures on it that
they found there.]

PATAECUS   Yes, I saw it then. (*Not looking at the piece
and struggling to rouse a dim memory*) And the next one,
wasn't it a goat or a bull or some such animal?

GLYCERA   It's a stag, my dear, not a goat.

PATAECUS   Something with horns, I remember that. And
the third one is a winged horse. (*Aside, and not overheard
by Glycera, who is preoccupied with the things in the chest,
in anguish*) These things are my wife's! My poor wife's!

(*Absorbed in what they are doing, they are unaware that
Moschion has come out of Myrrhina's house. He walks from
the door aimlessly and moodily, jolted by the new knowledge
that he is a foundling. After a moment he notices the two and,
unobserved, draws near. The piece of embroidery catches his
eye—and he steps back in astonishment on seeing that it is
identical with a piece that had, but a short while ago, been
shown to him as one of his birth tokens.*)

MOSCHION   (*aside, agitated*) When I see this (*gesturing toward the embroidery that Glycera is holding*) I can
only believe that my mother had a daughter, too, whom she
abandoned the same time she did me. And if this is what
happened, she's my sister and, heaven help me, I'm ruined!
(*Carefully concealing himself, he eavesdrops intently.*)

PATAECUS   (*in a daze at the melodramatic turn events
have taken, aside*) Oh, God! What do they mean, these relics
from my past?

GLYCERA   (*with no inkling of what her tokens convey to
Pataecus, and only concerned to prove that they are really
hers*) Go ahead and ask me anything you want about them.

PATAECUS   (*intensely*) Tell me, where did you get
these?

GLYCERA   They were found with me when I was an
infant.

MOSCHION   (*suddenly aware he had, in his excitement,
been edging closer and closer to them, to himself*) Back a

little! Moschion, you're on the crest of a wave headed right
for the crisis of your life!

PATAECUS   (*as before*)   Was it only you who was abandoned? (*Urgently*) Tell me!

GLYCERA   No. A brother was abandoned with me.

MOSCHION   (*aside*)   Ah—that's one of the things I
wanted to know.

PATAECUS   How did you become separated?

GLYCERA   I could tell you the whole story if I wanted;
I've heard it all. But, please, ask me only about myself because I can talk about that. I swore to her that I wouldn't
talk about the rest.

MOSCHION   (*aside*)   Another clue for me. Plain as day:
it's Myrrhina she swore to. (*Visibly shaken, he speaks un-
steadily.*) I've got to find my bearings. . . . (*He slumps down
to a seat and stares ahead vacantly, deaf for the moment
to what is going on about him.*)

PATAECUS   Who was it who took you and brought you
up?

GLYCERA   A woman found me lying there. She brought
me up.

PATAECUS   Did she ever mention where she found you?

GLYCERA   She mentioned a spring in a shady spot.

PATAECUS   (*dazedly, to himself*)   The very place he told
me about after he exposed them.

GLYCERA   (*caught up by Pataecus' words*)   Who was
that? If it's no secret, let me know too.

PATAECUS   (*slowly, uttering the words with visible effort*)   The one who exposed you was a slave. But the one
who refused to raise his own children . . . was . . . I.

(*He stands with head bowed and eyes averted. Glycera
stares at him. Her joy at discovering her father is for the
moment overbalanced by her sense of injury at the life she has
been forced into by his one and only act as a father.*)

GLYCERA   *You* exposed me? My own father! (*Agoniz-
edly*) Why, why?

PATAECUS   (*speaking in a low voice and, eschewing ordi-*

nary language, selecting his words with extreme care) My child, Fate does many incredible things. Your mother, soon after giving birth to you, left this life. And just the day before she died—

GLYCERA   What happened? Oh, I'm almost afraid to hear!

PATAECUS   I became a pauper—I who had always lived in comfort.

GLYCERA   In one day? Oh, god, how terrible! But how?

PATAECUS   I received the news that the ship which represented my whole livelihood had gone down in a storm in the Aegean.

GLYCERA   A terrible stroke of luck—for me!

PATAECUS   I thought that to try to raise two children, now that I was a beggar, was completely senseless, like trying to sail with a pair of anchors dragging. (*Both are silent for a moment.*) Do you have the rest of the things, my child?

GLYCERA   Which ones?

PATAECUS   Whatever was left with you.

GLYCERA   Let me list them. There were a necklace and a little jeweled adornment to identify us.

PATAECUS   Let's take a look at that. [A line and a half is lost here.]

MOSCHION   (*who has roused himself from his trance and is listening intently, aside*)   This man is my father!

PATAECUS   Could you give me some details?

GLYCERA   (*thinking*)   There was a purple belt.

PATAECUS   Yes, there was.

GLYCERA   With dancing girls embroidered on it.

MOSCHION   (*recognizing from the description one of his birth tokens, aside*)   So you know about that!

GLYCERA   And a woman's wrap of sheer fabric and a gold headband. There, I've listed them all.

PATAECUS   (*going toward her, his arms spread wide*) My dear girl, I can't restrain myself—

(*As Pataecus goes to embrace Glycera, Moschion rushes forward and reveals himself.*)

MOSCHION   (wildly) I . . . [A line and a half are lost
here.] I'm here . . .
PATAECUS   God in heaven! Who is this?

[At this dramatic climax there is a break of at least one
hundred lines. Moschion declared himself and there must have
been a highly charged rapprochement between father and
son, and protestations and explanations between brother and
sister. And Glycera's belongings must have made a second
trip, this time from Myrrhina's house to Pataecus'. Installing
Glycera there involved, naturally, dispossessing Polemon, and
he, in the course of being told why, learned of Glycera's great
good luck. The news plunged him into even deeper depths of
despair: in the light of her new rank, his brutal act seemed
worse than ever and his chances of getting her back even more
remote. When the text resumes, he is bewailing his sorry state
to Doris. We are now somewhere in Act. V.]

ACT V

(*Doris and Polemon are standing in front of his house. Polemon is in bad shape: he is drawn and haggard, his hair is unkempt, and his clothes are in utter disarray.*)

POLEMON   (*wildly*)   And so, I decided to hang myself!
DORIS   (*taking him seriously and horrified*)   No! You
mustn't!
POLEMON   (*as before*)   But what am I going to do,
Doris? Without Glycera what good is this miserable life of
mine?
DORIS   (*reassuringly*)   She'll come back to you.
POLEMON   (*shaking his head in a vigorous negative*)
Oh, god! You don't know what you're saying.
DORIS   She will—if you're ready and willing to behave
yourself from now on.
POLEMON   (*babbling with excitement*)   I will, I will.
I'll watch every step I make. My dear girl, you're right,
you're absolutely right. You go to her. Doris, I'll set you
free first thing tomorrow. Listen, here's what you've got to

say—(*As Doris turns and runs into Pataecus' house, to him-self*) She's gone in. Oh, Glycera, you've got me completely in your power! (*Paces up and down for a moment in silence. Then, with bitter self-recrimination*) It was no lover you kissed that time, it was your brother. And I was so jealous and hipped on getting even, I thought you were deceiving me and I went berserk on the spot. So, I was going to hang myself—and a good thing too. (*To Doris as she comes out of Pataecus' house, eagerly*) Doris, my girl! What's the news?

DORIS   (*excitedly*) It's good. She's coming out to see you.

POLEMON   (*incredulously*) She was joking.

DORIS   Lord, no! She's all dressed up. Her father can't take his eyes off her. You know what you ought to do? Arrange a party right now to celebrate her good luck and the happy ending of all these troubles!

POLEMON   (*enthusiastically*) By god, that's a great idea! My cook's inside; just came back from shopping. I'll have him prepare a pork roast.

DORIS   What about all the formal preliminaries?

POLEMON   (*energetically*) Preliminaries later. I want to get going on the pig. And I want to grab a garland from some altar and put it on.

DORIS   (*smiling as she observes his far from partylike general appearance*) That'll at least give you a more convincing look for the occasion.

POLEMON   You can bring her out now.

DORIS   Matter of fact, she'll be out any minute. Her father too.

POLEMON   (*nervous as a schoolboy*) He too? (*As the door of Pataecus' house starts to open*) Oh, my god! (*Loses his nerve completely and bolts into his house.*)

DORIS   (*calling after him*) Hey! What are you doing? (*To herself*) He's gone. What's so terrible about a door opening? Well, I'll go in too; maybe there's something I can lend a hand with.

(*Doris follows Polemon into his house. A moment later Gly-cera, elegantly dressed, and Pataecus enter.*)

PATAECUS   I was simply delighted when you said you
were willing to be reconciled. When you are riding high, to
be willing to accept what is fair—that's the mark of the
Greek character. (*To his slaves in the house*) Someone go
call Polemon.

POLEMON   (*bursting out from behind his door where he
had obviously been eavesdropping*)   I'm coming! (*He hurries over to them, then stands embarrassed and ill at ease.*)
I heard that Glycera had found the ones she was looking for,
so I was inside arranging a party to celebrate the good news.

PATAECUS   (*nodding   vigorously*)   You're   absolutely
right. Now listen to me; I have something to tell you. (*Solemnly*) Do you Polemon, take this woman for your lawfully
wedded wife?

POLEMON   (*promptly*)   I do.

PATAECUS   Her dowry is ninety thousand dollars.

POLEMON   Fine!

PATAECUS   (*warningly*)   From now on, forget that
you're a soldier. Absolutely no more of this going wild and
flying off the handle.

POLEMON   (*fervently*)   A man who missed ruin by a
hair to fly off the handle again? God, no! What's more, I'll
never even find any fault in my Glycera. (*Turning to her*)
Sweetheart! Are we reconciled?

GLYCERA   As it turned out, your going berserk was the
beginning of our happiness.

POLEMON   How true!

GLYCERA   And for that reason I forgive you.

POLEMON   (*turning to Pataecus*)   Pataecus, you'll come
to the party?

PATAECUS   There's another marriage I've got to look
after. I'm getting Philinus' daughter for my son.

MOSCHION   (*who has come out of his house just in time
to hear Pataecus' last statement*)   Oh, my god!

[The manuscript breaks off here, but we are almost certainly within a few lines of the end of the play.]